CROSS-COUNTRY SKIING IN NEW ENGLAND

"Just thumbing through the pages of this guidebook gives you the feeling that the authors have really explored the places they describe."

— Maine SUNDAY TELEGRAM

"Notes in its introduction that children are welcome at all of the ski areas included in the guide."

—FAMILY TRAVEL TIMES

"This book is the next best thing to a guide at your side."

—THE NEW ENGLAND SAMPLER, *Belfast, Maine*

CROSS-COUNTRY SKIING

IN NEW ENGLAND

Fourth Edition

by
Lyn and Tony Chamberlain

OLD SAYBROOK, CONNECTICUT

Photo Credits: Pp. ii, 127: Maine Nordic Ski Council; pp. vi, viii, x, xiii, xvi: Woodstock Inn & Resort; pp. viii, 23, 59, 65, 162: Mountain Top Inn & Resort; pp. 25, 33, 36, 53, 141, 155 by Ed Sawyer; p. 137: copyright ©1989 by Peter Miller (courtesy of the Trapp Family Lodge); all other photos by Janet Knott.

Cover and interior design by Nancy Freeborn
Cover photo by Ed Sawyer

Library of Congress Cataloging-in-Publication Data

Chamberlain, Lyn.
    Cross-country skiing in New England/by Lyn and Tony Chamberlain:— 4th ed.
        p.   cm.
    Includes index.
    ISBN 1-56440-837-X
    1. Cross-country skiing—New England—Guidebooks. 2. New England—Guidebooks. I. Chamberlain, Tony. II. Title.
    GV854.5.N35C45 1995
    917.404'43—dc20   95-34929
                                                        CIP

Manufactured in the United States of America
Fourth Edition/Second Printing

for Earl and Hobie,
with our love

CONTENTS

PROLOGUE:

ONE OF TOO FEW DAYS

It was nearly 4 A.M. and the wind was down. Whatever had woken me—there were mice in this place, we knew—was still now. I went over to the window and pulled back the wool blanket we had tacked against the cold early last evening. When we turned in, a storm was raging across the valley, so the window was just a flat black. But sometime in the night the weather had blown itself out. Now, over the still silver landscape, hung a solemn January moon. I knew in a few hours one of Those Days was going to dawn.

There are too few such days in a winter; too few in a lifetime. The world remade by new snow, bright sun in an endless sky (for the high pressure was surely locked in for a while), and no commitment beyond a full day's skiing. It would be perfect. Even anticipating such a day, knowing how brief and finite it would be, brought a peculiar sense of dread to underline the exhilaration as I stood there at the window. I thought thoughts that look grotesquely sentimental on paper:

"This would be a day to be tuned to every minute, to resist that all-too-human habit of blocking off the senses, of losing awareness so that hours of light slip by uncounted, practically unnoticed.

"That may be okay back in the work world, sitting in commuter traffic or something of the kind. But not this day. This day would be perfect, every minute of it to be turned over and over, examined, savored."

Three hours later the moon was down and the first streak of hard orange light slashed across the peak of Bald Mountain. Bacon

and coffee smells filled the cabin; during twenty years of marriage, these two chores—the spadework of our vacation breakfasts—have fallen to me. Then Lyn, the superstar surgeon who can flip fried eggs without breaking them, steps in for the artistic work.

You can eat a big breakfast before a day of skiing, for the sport burns calories like none other I know. We were staying at a friend's camp in northern Maine, and the plan was to ski 12 miles to a village at the far shore of the lake, then cross the lake for a 4-mile shot home. After breakfast, as Lyn packed a trail lunch, I went about the ceremonial business of determining the wax of the day.

I have been with ski groups who delight in arguing all through breakfast about waxing, various members going out every five minutes to stick a thermometer in sunlit snow, then in the shady snow, then to stand around ruminatively stroking their chins while pretending to know a great deal about winter. My own experience is that for recreational touring you can be a color or so off to the cold side and it really won't matter much, especially if your touch on the skis is right. All it will really mean is that you herringbone up-hill a little sooner than you would otherwise. And you can be more than a color off to the warm side before you start clogging up your kick zone.

I used some paint thinner to remove some old grip wax from the green glider base we'd ironed on the fiber glass bottoms at the beginning of the season, then on the kick zone I smeared some green grip wax—just a guess on my part about what would be a good start in this dry, fluffy stuff.

Anyway, as long as waxing stays ceremonial, it is fun. So the skis were prepared on our perfect morning; lunch, waxes, extra clothes packed in the back pack, and off we went.

The empty woods on a cold morning ring with quiet. The powder was still unbroken as we made our way up behind the cabin, mounting toward a high ridge that ran for about 3 miles overlooking the lake. The only breaks in the trail were the delicate strings of beads, the tracks of small animals—squirrels, snowshoe hare, voles, and the like—up and busy in these hills long before us. During a blizzard, deer will hunker down in the snow and become buried for the duration. When they sense the storm's end, they will break out to continue their ceaseless winter foraging for food, and you sometimes come upon their tracks on winter mornings after a snowfall. You are reminded that northern New England is the extreme range of whitetail deer; in the deepest months the animals are always in peril.

As you stretch out, skiing faster through the dark hollows and over small rises—always ascending—the muscles work out, and the stiffness of beginning is gone. Skiing becomes easier. You are in rhythm and are aware of your sound; skis patting, then gliding on the snow, your breath coming out in plumes as your lungs work to drink the winter-cold oxygen. Rhythm, the slash-slash of skis, the steamy breath, and suddenly you become aware of how loud the sound of your skiing is in this early silence.

Still in shade, we made one slight descent, then turned uphill again through a stand of birch and snow-laden fir boughs. I chose one route up here; Lyn said she would skirt around through another likely looking road that would be better going and would meet me at the other side of a knoll I was already ascending.

"I think my way's shorter," I told her.

"It's too thick-looking up there. I'm taking the road," she said, and we parted company.

I was determined to get over the knoll, then ski back down the road, to be waiting there not even breathing hard, as if I'd been there for half the morning when she showed up. Skiing harder up toward the rise, I had to duck under several branches so heavily laden they looked ready to snap. As my shoulder brushed by, unburdening them, the boughs sprung one by one toward the sky, spraying me with powder.

Toward the top of a mountain ridge, summer or winter, when you emerge from thick woods to a spacious overlook, there is a sense of climbing out a skylight onto the roof of the world. Here, abruptly, I was in sunlight, full and dazzling. Far below, the lake spread out for 10 miles, a pool of spilled milk. Beyond one shore, the tiny village stoked its fires in the cold morning, the thin curls of smoke rising from every rooftop into the valley air. Even farther beyond the lake and village rose another mountain ridge, then another a fainter blue behind it, and another behind that. Looking out over moutain ranges, you can see the tumultuous energy of a frozen ocean. And as far as I could see, perhaps 80 miles, just visible behind the last ridge rose the oddly sinister white bulk of Mountain Katahdin.

It was some time before I noticed there was no way down from where I stood. The underbrush among the firs down the sunny side of the ridge was waist-high and so thick there was no apparent opening. But I was not about the backtrack to the road, then skirt all the way around, following Lyn by perhaps fifteen minutes. I drove down through the underbrush and commenced such a fight with the thickets that, after ten minutes or so, I was more amused than irritated. I would hack an opening and make a move through it, only to find that one ski was so hung up around a stalk or some creeper vines that I must back up again, then look to the other ski to see what it was doing. Meanwhile, I had to duck under the heavy fir boughs that kept dumping their powder over my shoulders and head. Just as I was losing a ridiculous battle with these woods, I was at last free and worked down to the road. As I arrived, snow-covered, disheveled, steaming and panting from the effort, there was Lyn looking as if she'd been waiting there all morning. No explanation was necessary. "How's the other guy look?" she asked.

We found a patch of sunlight to stop in. After two hours of skiing, it was time to shed a layer and have some coffee and Hershey chunks, before pushing on to our lunch stop. We descended half a mile to the lake. Where the downhill run was clear, it was exhilarating, for we could let out the skis as fast as we could travel through powder, then slow down naturally as the terrain leveled. But it did occur to me that going downhill on skinny skis is not as much fun as going up gentle climbs, or over flats. And this is a matter of sheer skiing skill, or lack thereof: You can learn to charge over flats and pump uphill and get the same exhilarating high that distance runners feel. But the ability to ride a ski downhill with confidence through twisting terrain and switchbacks—that is a matter of years and miles under the skis. For that there is no substitute.

Our lunch was hot soup from a wide-mouth Thermos, chicken chunks, bread, cheese, and wine to wash it down. Now the sun was high and flooded into our small clearing. I peeled off a layer and sat there steaming, pointing my face stupidly to the sky. Odd, wasn't it? Here in the heart of winter—the darkest month in one of the fiercest climates in North America—it was possible to peel off layers of clothing, sip wine, and nearly doze in the sunshine. But shadows begin to elongate quickly on a January day. After half an hour or so there was a sudden nudge of urgency. Get going. We picked up, smeared a touch of blue wax over the green, and were off again, feeling stiff and cranky, along the shore of the lake.

We were getting near civilization now. The first sign was the waste of raw material from which the outlanders—beavers—had built winter communes. They had built two huge lodges just off-shore of the lake, and all along the shore lay the ruins of birch trees they had felled for the construction. A wasteful project, this, for the beavers used only medium logs and small limbs, leaving the greater part of the tree sprawled on the forest floor to rot. And how much more wasteful, it seems, when the waste is birch. Scattered among these stands of beech, maple, and birch were silver birches, the prettiest trees I have seen, their trunks shining a bright gold-bronze color, bright as polished metal in the chilly sunlight.

We passed out of beaver country and began coming upon the most common of lodgings in ski country, the ubiquitous, inevitable condominium. With the first ones we passed, we knew, despite the last part of our trip ahead of us—a straight shot home across the lake after picking up groceries—The Day was at its end.

And the run home, our dividend, was nearly uneventful except for the hugest of events. Two of them.

Loaded down with two extra packs stuffed with all kinds of un-necessaries for the rest of our week up-country, we headed back across the lake just as the sun diffused in the broad florid band across the western sky, an unconvincing final show of force before the winter night shut down over all light once again. It was comfort-able on the lake. There was no wind. Skiers had left behind plenty of tracks for us to get into and cruise along, and the dropping tempera-ture made the surface firm and fast. And again there was the exhila-ration of the aerobic rhythm, the rhythm of motion and breathing, that slash-slash of the skis. We were across in no time.

We ascended the opposite banking crossing a neighbor's meadow in the dark, then up past his barn where a solitary white cat dozed on a window ledge under the outside light. Then into the dark again, through more trees to the last field we would have to cross to get back to our cabin. At the edge of the clearing there was movement of some kind. Startled, I stared at something large and dark moving against the trees. The movement was not rushed, but slow and weighty. I was stunned. I tried to focus on an oft-repeated belief of an old Vermonter who taught me how to fly-fish: "The only animal you have to worry about in the New England woods stands on two legs."

Then I thought the neighbor's cows or perhaps his horses were loose. But the apparition finally resolved itself into a couple of moose sauntering along at the edge of the woods. If our sudden presence stirred them into motion, they certainly were not hurried about anything now. Their heads looking naked without antlers—the winter style for these thousand-pound monsters—they slowly shuffled toward the trees. Moose are the only creatures in New England for whom winter absolutely does not exist. I have seen them from an airplane lying on their backs and wriggling back and forth in the snow like horses in summer mud. Where the whitetailed deer are constantly threatened up here, these huge cousins do not even feel the pinch.

We heard their hooves plunge lazily a few times, then the noise stopped. The moose had stopped just a few yards into the trees and would wait for us to pass on before coming back to the clearing. It is no wonder hunters have a 90-percent success ratio up here with these brutes.

We crossed the last field, slowly and sorely now; day's end was suddenly long overdue. Halfway across the field we could see that the friends we'd expected sometime that evening had already arrived and were waiting for us. The windows were full of light. You could see wood smoke from the chimney against the stars.

INTRODUCTION

This book has been assembled with the single purpose of enhancing the pleasure of cross-country skiers in their sport by pointing them in certain directions. It by no means pretends to be a skiing bible. It does not get especially technical in questions of technique, and it even waffles on the question of whether to buy waxable or waxless skis. Its waxing approach is clearly for the lazy. It does not tell you how to skate or double-pole. It does not even attempt to suggest that descending steep turny downhills on Nordic skis will ever be anything but a terror for you.

No, these pages have been assembled by a couple of folks who love the sport of skiing in all its facets, who love the rural reaches of New England and who hardly miss a winter weekend getting there, and who now share with you a few of the things they have found out.

ABOUT THIS BOOK

This is a guidebook for skiers and has been written for the skier, not the ski area. That is to say, the descriptions of ski areas herein are as faithful to the experience as we could make them. Prospective skiers may be influenced by what they read here to try this touring center or that one because it rings a particular note of appeal. That is the intent of this book.

Certain information may be lacking. Price, for instance. As you look at the statistical top half of an area's description, you will not find price. That is only partly because we hope this book outlives the price changes of one or two years. More to the point, within a

95-percent range of all the areas, prices are all about the same: They fall between $5.00 and $10.00 for a day's trail pass. Rental equipment ranges from $12.00 to $25.00.

Two other near universals: There are no areas where children are unwelcome; there are no areas where pets are welcome.

Unlike many Alpine areas that make a selling point of the fact that they operate a nursery for toddlers, this is hardly ever the case with Nordic areas. Exceptions will be noted in the narrative section in the lower half of the description.

Dogs? Leave them home, period. You may have a romantic picture in your mind of coursing through the pristine woodlands with Rover leaping along beside you. Save this for woods and wilderness touring of your own making. But when visiting a commercial touring center, especially one with groomed and trackset trails, leave the beasties home. Aside from ruining the track as they run along, dogs will inevitably blunder into the path of another skier (especially on double tracks), and send that skier out of control, or worse, unwittingly knock him over. No fair. Dogs stay home.

A word about trail difficulty. The nomenclature has changed over the years, and the current terms "easiest, more difficult, most difficult" have been thoughtfully chosen by the Professional Ski Instructors of America (PSIA). They replace the earlier "beginner, intermediate, expert" for two important reasons. First, these earlier terms were an attempt to describe the skiers who should use such trails, not the trails themselves. Secondly, no one knows exactly what the terms really mean. What is the difference, please, between an "advanced intermediate" and a newly arrived "expert," or an "experienced beginner"?

The new terms attempt to describe, in a relative way, the difficulty of a particular trail. If a trail system offers "most difficult" terrain, that means it is more difficult than its second-degree terrain, "more difficult." This latter is more difficult than the "easiest" terrain at the particular area, but not necessarily at all areas.

The trail-grooming entry attempts to let a skier know what sort of a playing surface to expect. A groomed trail means that some device or other—perhaps just a snowmobile—has passed over the raw snow and packed it down, making it generally a bit faster and easier to ski than a nongroomed trail. A *trackset* is just what it says. By pulling another device over the snow, a firm, well-defined track is set to ski in. This makes the skiing easier and faster and is sought by folks who like to "run" on their skis. On tracks it is easier to concentrate on what your body is doing rather than the terrain.

Double trackset means at least two tracks have been set, one beside another. This works just like automobile traffic (with the exception of one-way loops). Faster skiers pull out to pass slower ones; skiers from opposite directions pass without having to get out of a track. There is nothing less courteous, by the way, than two companion skiers coming abreast of one another, using both tracks, and forcing a skier from the opposite direction out of his right-hand track. Very gauche, but it is mentioned here because it happens.

Skating means that at least some of the skiable terrain at the area has been prepared in the wide, smooth lanes needed by skaters. Skating is fairly well established now so that almost all areas accommodate both styles, with the exception of those few that describe themselves as "wilderness" or non-grooming areas.

Under the instruction entry, PSIA-certified stands for Professional Ski Instructors of America. If the notation is made this way it means that your instructor has had to prove to other professional instructors that he knows what he is doing and teaches according to a method recognized and used by all others in PSIA. It is an indication that you will have a skilled teacher.

The converse, however, is decidely not true. Merely because a teacher is noncertified is no indication that he is not just as good as a certified instructor. So don't weigh this category too heavily, except to note whether any instruction is available.

On rentals, we have noted, where possible, how many sets are available. Some areas simply chose not to tell us how many they had, while others gave us detailed rundowns on the state-of-the-art binding systems. One rule of thumb anywhere, however: If you're going to rent, show up early. This is obviously true of the busier areas but should be standard practice anyway. Arriving later may mean you're forced into compromises like skis too long and boots too small. No fun. One alternative to explore is renting equipment at the ski shop near your home and taking it with you. This way you'll also avoid the brutal Saturday-morning crush in the rental store.

To know where you're going, use the state map. Find the number of the touring center you plan to visit. The number refers to the map index giving you the page number where the area is described.

Between the description in the book and the routes on the map, most places will be easy to find. But frequent visitors to New England's rural reaches should also be armed with full-scale, detailed road maps.

Two final notes: First to skiers, this book is written for you. Write and give us feedback. Tell us where you think we blew it. Maybe we glowed too much, or not enough. Perhaps you found some feature worth noting at an area that we missed. The only way we'll ever know is if you drop us a line c/o The Globe Pequot Press, P.O. Box 833, Old Saybrook, CT 06475.

To the touring centers, if you have made changes or improvements that we should know about, or if we have overlooked an important feature of your center that you feel should be included, likewise, drop us a line.

And to any touring center not included herein, understand that this book is not advertising. No touring center has paid to be listed in this book. If you wish to be considered for a future edition, please write and let us know you're out there.

All that said, we repeat the hope that this guide to skiing in New England will accomplish our single goal of contributing to the pleasures of the marvelous sport of cross-country skiing.

A FEW MISCONCEPTIONS

In the autumn of 1984 Russian archaeologists found a ski near Soviet Georgia carbon-dated to an age of 4,000 B.C. That find displaced by a thousand years a Norwegian ski previously believed to be the oldest in existence. Whatever competitive spirit may exist over what country owns the oldest ski, the real point is that in frigid climes man has probably been on skis as long as he has used his feet. Beyond mere amusement or exercise regimen, the simple fact is that skiing is the fastest, easiest, and natural way to travel over the snow-covered earth.

Not that the sport needs a defense. Indeed, cross-country skiing, with all its names and variants—ski touring, Nordic, Norpine, Telemarking—is here for a good long stay. It has that winning formula: cheap, simple, healthy, and fun. Its importance to a modern human who increasingly searches for ways to bring nature into his recreational and exercise life makes skiing nearly as significant as it was to ancient man.

For more than a decade in our country, cross-country skiing has redoubled several times in popularity. The sport is now an established, solid, growing, thriving, and incredibly healthful endeavor. But a few old misconceptions still remain.

NUMBER ONE: *It's too much work.*

Well, for starters, how much work is too much work? Some people believe cross-country skiing is in the running family—that if they can't imagine themselves jogging 5 miles a day, then they're disqualified from cross-country skiing.

Not so. Running, aside from the well-documented jarring involved, is an all-or-nothing sort of regimen. That is, either one is running or one is not running. If one is not running he is walking or standing still. If he is running, no matter how slowly, he is under terrific stress—the whole point of the sport. His only way out is to stop, and then he is not running anymore.

Skiing is very different in that regard. In its recreational mode it is much more like bicycling. One can bike at a hundred beats a minute in the Tour de France, or one can coast and cruise. Pump five strokes, then let the legs rest as the eyes take in the countryside. Skiing can be done exactly this way, from a vigorous running pace to a leisurely cruise with lots of coasting. To be utterly frank, though, if an easy-to-moderately-paced bike ride is too much work for you, then, yes, cross-country skiing is probably not for you, either.

NUMBER TWO: *It's boring.*

This is easier. Anyone who gets bored with the winter wilderness outside those walls, with the dazzle of sun on snow-white and evergreen, is simply bored with himself, bored with life, we think. Cross-country skiing won't help.

NUMBER THREE: *If you can walk you can cross-country ski.*

We have seen too many people disappointed by this amiably misguided notion to let it go unanswered. There is a minimal amount of truth here to be sure. The phrase is generally repeated to assure novices that Nordic skiing has nothing of the slam-bang recklessness they perceive in downhill skiing.

In some ways this is true, but it is only true because you begin to cross-country ski on flat terrain. Move the legs in a walking sort of way, and you will move forward. No problem. But somewhere along the way one of two things will happen. The new skier will eventually encounter the need to go up, down, or sideways—situations that call for more concentration than your average after-dinner walk. Or, as he steps along, another skier will go by him on the trail so fast he looks motor-driven. Actually, this skilled skier looks like a little machine put together with elastic bands and pendulums: everything rhythmic, easy, and—oh Lord!—so fast.

Once the new cross-country skier sees what real skiing is like, he endeavors to go faster, mainly because the faster you go on skis the more fun you have. But it takes more skill to go fast, as well as some practice and experience. It is here that cross-country skiing departs the realm of walking. Oh, it is still as leisurely as the skier wants it to be. But once the bug gets into the advanced beginner's head that springing across flat tracks at 15 miles an hour looks like fun, well, in our judgment that is the real gateway to cross-country fun. And it sure isn't walking then.

How to get from here to there?

That's the easiest question in the book. Take a lesson. Get a certified professional to teach you. Not in big doses. But half an hour here, half an hour there. The practice in-between times—pleasant miles under the skis—is the key to progressing. Keep in mind, however, that you do not have to progress, but you will most likely want to improve your skills. You need never feel compelled to be anything beyond a woods-walker, an air-sniffer, and birdsong-listener. Indeed, we should all remember that this is primal in the joy of ski touring.

We have seen at least two distinct kinds of malaise develop over this matter of skiing proficiency or skill. One day we took a friend skiing for the first time. He was an athlete, a marathon runner, and a sometime Alpine skier in terrific physical condition. As our appointed date at the Weston Ski Track approached, we made the mistake of sloughing off my friend's real concerns about his first experience with skinny skis.

Would it feel awkward? Would he fall down a lot? Hurt himself?

"Are you kidding?" we would say, "An athlete in your condition, who has good downhill experience? You'll pick it up like that."

Our afternoon at Weston was a disaster. Not that our friend fell all over the place, hurt himself, or hyperventilated in fatigue, mind you. No, cross-country skiing was merely a maddening frustration for him.

At the Weston track there are always a few expert runners in training who make 20 miles an hour over the flats look easy. And of course, given our advanced promotion, along with our friend's expectation that he could master Nordic skiing immediately, well . . . disaster is the word. He teetered unsurely, tried with determination to take off at top speed, and just never got over feeling off-balance and rather foolish. A conspicuous failure. The worst of it was he wanted to look like the experts, wanted to go just as fast. He thought he should be able to and just could not understand why it didn't come to him at once. He has not been skiing since.

The second type of malaise developed in someone we know who did not want to go fast, who did not want to run through courses, who cared not a fig about double-poling and less about skating. If a hill looked less like a challenge than a chore, she would opt for the route around it. Or at least she would climb it slowly and under protest.

What she loved most about skiing was the solitude, the utter porcelain beauty of the winter landscape, the tracks of wild animals crossing the trail, the difference between white and silver birch. This woman was (dubiously) blessed with a husband and two sons who were jocks. Every minute on skis was a contest with each other or any surrounding bit of landscape. Every ski trip became, rather than a tour in remote wilderness beauty, a challenge. Where she did not want to run up a hill, they prodded her with the old, "It'll feel good when you get up there."

The challenges the males of this family found fun and exciting were merely obstacles to the woman's enjoyment. She had a feeling they all moved so fast they couldn't possibly take in their surroundings.

But, you say, understanding this is merely human courtesy or sensitivity.

Yes, of course, as was true in the first case. Still, these are two examples we've seen played out repeatedly. Which is why we invariably suggest that the beginner go straight to a qualified professional instructor. The pro will find out what you know about skiing, what you expect from the sport, and where you want to go. And, he can reassure you that you needn't go anywhere you do not choose to go. He will encourage you to progress at your own pace so you do not frustrate yourself trying to accomplish things you're not ready for.

Friends and relatives who know something about the sport can be helpful, but the truth is they often are not. Often, in fact, they make the cardinal mistake of trying to teach too much, and this leads to serious trouble. Go with the pro. Learn a couple of things here and there to work on when you're skiing at your leisure. And—most important at times—declare yourself to those around you. Don't be bullied into skiing over your head.

TO THE DOWNHILL SKIER

That cross-country skiing has long outlived its critics as a popular sport is no historical accident. The fact is that cross-country skiing predates Alpine skiing by eons.

For starters, despite the electric thrill of Alpine skiing, the Nordic version has the advantage of being cheaper, more accessible, more sociable, better exercise, and certainly less crowded. Have you ever stood in a line to take off across a field or golf course for a morning cross-country run?

Not that this book intends to make a judgment of one over the other. Certainly, any skier who understands the heritage of the skimeister gives equal dignity to all forms of the sport. What is best about the ski age we live in is that we need not choose one over the other. The thrill of downhill skiing at high speed with those sure, crisp, steel-edged turns is undeniable. But if the last two decades have proved anything in the entire world of skiing it is that Nordic, cross-country, ski touring, running—whatever term you use to identify the sport—is surely as exciting in its own right and needn't be apologized for as "the alternative."

At the National Cross-Country Championships at Bretton Woods, New Hampshire, in 1982, Tony asked Bill Koch, that year's World Cup winner, what seemed at the time an overly simplistic question: "What separates the winners from the near-winners in this sport of cross-country? Training? Determination? The right wax?"

Koch thought for a moment, assessing his season, then answered in his characteristically humble way. "I've been doing well on the downhill sections," he said.

His coach, Mike Gallagher, explained more fully. All the skiers in the very top of a world-class field are in peak condition. They've probably waxed the same, and surely all of them on that level are lion-hearted athletes. But Koch's success that year came from his greatness as a downhill skier. Touch, technique, the way he rode his skis so aggressively into turns, flying downhill without the slightest tendency to hold back—it was the great downhiller in Koch that made the great skier and champion.

On the very next day, after the races, a gang of us went up to try the Bretton Woods NASTAR course on an Alpine slope. We were on Alpine skis. The clear winner among us through twenty-five slalom gates was Craig Ward, a member of the U.S. Nordic team who did the course on cross-country skis. And his were not the steel-edged, fatter compromise called a Norpine ski, either. Ward had skied the course on his light, stiff racing skis that usually require an act of God for us ordinary skiers to turn.

The point is that skiing is skiing is skiing. The division one supposes to exist between Nordic and Alpine forms is at best a thin cultural bias carried on by crabby folks who don't really understand skiing in its broadest sense.

We are in an age of such increasing expense in Alpine skiing that mixing the forms up is becoming ever more popular for the weekend ski family. It's a natural: A day of downhill, a day of cross-country. Actually, the other way around is probably better, since Saturdays are usually more crowded at Alpine areas than are Sundays.

What most downhill skiers find is that rather than a cheap pastime as an alternative, Nordic is a workout that requires the same principles of balance, counter-rotation of the body, leaning well out over the skis, knees bent in the weight transfer of a Telemark turn. And beyond mere technical differences, Nordic skiing has its own rhythm and beauty, a kind of pendular symmetry the Alpine aficionado finds hauntingly familiar.

Several of the Nordic centers described in this book are combined with Alpine areas. From Stowe, Vermont to Waterville Valley, New Hampshire, to Kingfield, Maine, and the Sugarloaf environs, to Berkshire East in Massachusetts—wherever you find Alpine skiing there are bound to be some Nordic tracks nearby.

And so here is an invitation to any downhiller who one day feels just a bit down in the checkbook, who dreads another half-hour liftline, who is sick of fussing with forty pounds of gear, who cannot bear one more chairlift ride of subarctic wind chills, and who just may long for a day of utter solitude in the winter woods of New England: Give Nordic a try. You can rent gear and buy trail maps, lunch, and a starter lesson all for about the price of a lift ticket. And you just might gain some skills that will make you a better downhiller.

Come on and give it a try. What do you have to lose but your prejudices?

BEYOND THE GOOD NEWS

If there is a religious zeal among some cross-country skiiers—and we're sure there is—then get ready for the real good news about the sport. We've always known cross-country skiing is good for body as well as soul. But how good?

Rising head and shoulders above the current wave of fitness gurus (despite her rather diminutive stature) is Jackie Sorenson, who did as much as anyone to popularize aerobic conditioning. Sorenson's facts have never been in question. Here is her latest calorie line on various physical regimens. If you're a 125-pound person (extrapolate for your weight) then thirty minutes of moderate walking will burn about 125 calories. If you can swim thirty yards per minute, you'll burn 175 calories in the same half hour; ditto for ice-skating.

Golf will take care of 160 calories per half hour, and moderate biking will burn 175, too, though strenuous biking will take care of 275. Now hiking: 185 calories per half hour. Good fast walking: 230. Into the rough stuff. Racquetball: 350 per half hour, with running pushing close to that figure, depending on how hard you pump the legs, of course.

We're sure you've guessed what's on the very top of this list. The heaviest calorie-burning sport of them all is that four-legged running routine called cross-country skiing. Per half hour, for a 125-pound person (a little person, really) the burn is 500 calories, with the effect all aerobic athletes know well—a high-calorie burn for up to four hours after the activity has stopped.

The explanation: Legs contain the vast bulk of muscle in the human body, and so the most energy is spent in vigorously exercising them. Now add to the legs, the next-largest groups—shoulders, chest, and arm muscles. Get them all working simultaneously and you have the highest calorie-burner of all, cross-country skiing. It's a little like running on all fours.

OFF TO THE RACES

As we explored earlier, cross-country skiing appeals on many levels. When Bill Koch won the 1982 World Cup, followed not far behind by such bright lights as Tim and Jennifer Caldwell, Dan

Simoneau, and others, it seemed that a topflight ski-racing tradition had finally taken root in America. Subsequent years proved that our early optimism was just that and that the United States is still perhaps five or six generations behind the Europeans—Swedes and Finns most notably.

Yet the Koch years did much for the sport as a sport, the competitive level beyond recreational cruising. Among other things, they raised the consciousness of recreational skiers that, as in running, anyone who can ski can race. And anyone and everyone can ski.

So at one end of the sport is the purely leisure-oriented, relaxed recreationalist. His love is moving slowly through the winter snows and taking his time with his surroundings. That is the skiing most people understood up until the late 1970s when, for a lack of a better term, the Koch years were upon us. Racers, we learned, did not come out of some special school for the very hot. Indeed, most fast skiers were skiers who skied a lot, got in shape, and knew the discipline.

Again, as with running, though not everyone is blessed with equal talents, anyone can get in shape and learn to ski well enough to race. And this is the marvelous prospect of citizen ski racing: It is there for anyone who wants it.

Along the Ellis River Trail in the Jackson, New Hampshire, system there is a measured 200-meter section for skiers to time themselves. We once waited near the end of that stretch to watch how many skiers were actually working on their times. On this intermediate-level trail, out of a dozen skiers there were ten who ran across the line huffing and puffing and looking at their watches.

Call it the American way, call it competitive instinct, or just allow that there is a natural delight in going fast on skis; the fact is, most skiers would love to race if they could. It is just human nature, once we rise to a certain level of proficiency, to want to test ourselves against a standard. Almost all the major ski-touring centers have citizen races that can be entered for a fee of about a buck. On one level these races are merely fun; on another level they elevate the sport of cross-counrty skiing to an unimaginable height.

Yes, citizen racing has become equivalent to road-running races, and there are several important analogies. Foremost, to beat a point into the ground, is this: Racing is for everyone and anyone. The hot shots go out and duel for the top one-hundred spots, while the duffer may just like rounding the course to stop at the feed stations. Most skiers are somewhere in the middle. Their contest is against the course, and they're in quest of that old Personal Best.

Races vary from 2-kilometer sprints to 50-kilometer marathons. Nearly all of them are open registration. The United States Ski Association (USSA) has several race series across the country, from 10-kilometer runs to the Great American Ski Chase Series.

One of the really fun races around is the annual Stowe Derby. Here, skiers take off from the top of Mount Mansfield, descend the fire trail for about 2,000 feet (a shallow descent, really), then run the remaining 10 miles into the town of Stowe, Vermont. Like most citizen races, this is low-key. Many skiers make the run for the wonderful social climate before and during the race and the beer blast afterward.

Aside from ordinary citizen touring, there are all kinds of kinky variations, such as Telemark races, downhill competitions dedicated to that artistic turn invented a century ago by Sondre Nordheim.

Then there is ski orienteering (Ski-O), a race through the wilderness in which skiers must also navigate with a compass and topographical map to find the course. This type of skiing has its roots in ancient military skills. Messengers from the Swedish or Finnish armies would have to find their way across the tundra to deliver crucial information. Thus, performance skiing and woodsmanship were equally tested, for going fast meant little in the wilderness if the messenger didn't know where he was going.

Then there's biathlon, triathlon, Nordic combined, and jumping—though these are rather specialized skills for the average weekend skier. Nevertheless, competition abounds everywhere and on every level of seriousness. Nearly every large area has a school with all the information you'll need for the current season in this region. Or, simply ask at the desk of an area where you're skiing. Most likely there will be notices posted about upcoming citizen events.

If improvement is one of your skiing goals, regardless of your current level, there is perhaps no faster path to better performance than learning the disciplines of competitive skiing.

And doesn't that cold drink taste good after a race!

THAT QUESTION: WAX

To start with an answer, I use both myself. How's that for a hedge?

The question: Who should use a no-wax ski, and who should wax?

I have heard so many sermons on this subject from so many sources that I am often reminded of two political parties in a campaign. Or two fishermen talking about the right fly to use in a stream.

I am also reminded of a heavy-bicycle/light-bicycle analogy. A fellow who runs a nearby bike shop was trying to sell a lightweight French racing bike to a customer who had come into the shop with his sights quite a bit lower. The customer asked what the French racing bike (at nearly twice the money) would do for him that the plainer, cheaper, heavier bike would not do.

"You can't even compare them," said the bike dealer. "It's just another level of the sport. The XYZ bike is more responsive and much much faster. It's another world."

Aside from the fact that the bike salesman had said nothing to really enlighten this customer, he left himself wide open and had utterly no response to the buyer's powerful truth:

"I'm interested in exercise and riding with my family on vacation," said the fellow. "What does it matter how fast I can go?"

If this describes exactly your attitude toward cross-country skiing, as I know it does for many, then go with the no-wax or waxless skis. (Then put a thin protective coat of glider wax on them anyway.)

Here are some other checkpoints for those who should probably go waxless:

. . . If you're an infrequent skier, half a dozen days or less in an average winter.

. . . If it drives you mad to slip backward, even a little bit, going uphill. And you hate to herringbone.

. . . If you live (and ski) in a part of the world where snow conditions vary greatly.

. . . If you hate equipment maintenance of all kinds, and waxing skis strikes you as fussy, scary, and/or stupid.

. . . If the thing you like best about jogging is the simplicity of putting on the shoes and walking out your door.

By these last checkpoints, do not get the idea that waxing is an overly laborious or time-consuming job. I know one certified teacher who goes for an hour's ski run every morning before teaching. His waxing method is to look at the thermometer and then to spend less than five minutes waxing his skis before his run. It is his well-founded belief that if being off by a color really jiggles a skier (unless he is racing), then there's something wrong in his technique.

But back to the waxless skier. As I say, I use both. My waxless skis are mid-thickness Trak Pacers. They are not lightweight, nor are they heavy trucks. The ridge pattern that gives them grip runs over a kick zone of moderate length. In other words, these are mid-everything skis. They'd be right for everyone except the competition skier or that highly experienced runner who likes the feel of flying with wings on his feet.

Much of my casual cross-country skiing begins at my back door. I'll get in an hour or more daily when the snow is good. I ski for a couple of miles through unpathed, hilly woods, ducking through occasional underbrush, then I emerge on a bridle path that circles a horse farm, cross through a broad tree farm beside it, running down through rows of evergreens that make me feel a little like a rat in a maze. Then I pop clear on a lovely eighteen-hole golf course, of which I can digest as much or as little as I have time for before I plunge back into the woods for the trek home.

If the snow is new and deep, I will most likely take the waxless skis. Their size and weight make them easier to break trail with, and I'm not so likely to break one on the jagged woods' floor. Though I'm interested, from an exercise point of view, in keeping a good aerobic pace going, speed per se is not my goal in such conditions. Waxless skis are the choice.

But there is another sort of day. The snow has settled and "set up." In the previous days I have skied tracks into my course, and it may even be a bit firm and fast today. I am not planning any exploratory forays off through unfamiliar woods, and I have a notion to run a few miles—that is, to ski at as fast a pace as I can, to get a nice rhythmic diagonal stride going, to huff and puff a bit.

Or I am at a touring center with trails groomed and trackset. Again, my purpose is to work out, to ski fast and steadily for at least half an hour before a break. In these latter instances, I'll use my pair of skinny, very light and stiff Jarvinen racing skis. Exactly why, when I'm not in a competition of any kind, is hard to say, but it comes down to a matter of feel. The light skinny skis—waxed close to correctly so you're not slipping backward or picking up balls of snow on the kick zone—somehow encourage the skier to go at it a bit more intensely. He leans out over the skis more, throws his hip more into the stride, the pole hand reaching further out and up as he settles into that nice easy rhythm that looks nearly effortless though it produces maximum speed.

Of course, the same pleasing rhythm of the diagonal stride can be performed on waxless skis as well. But the lightweight waxed ski heightens that pleasure to the extreme. The feet feel nearly weightless as the skis glide faster and faster over the snow, and now the skier is into that often-overlooked element in cross-country skiing—speed. And speed on skis reads fun.

This is not to suggest that everyone go buy two pairs of skis simply to explore the extreme range of the sport. But for someone who plans to spend plenty of winter hours working out on skis in the way described above—skiing tracks and predictable terrain—and who finds the prospect of messing around with waxes sort of fun, or at least not disagreeable, then a pair of waxable skis may be in order.

As I said at the outset, this is a rather hedged answer. I own two pairs of skis to prove it.

If you have skied several times on your waxless skis and want to feel the difference, try a demo. Most of the larger touring centers will have most varieties of skis on hand. And if it is clear you are taking a demo run, many rental shops will wax the skis for you and give you a complimentary hour on them. This may also be a good time for some instruction, for lightweight waxed skis are not quite as forgiving of sloppy technique as are most waxless skis.

WAXING UP

So you've decided to go with a pair of waxable skis: Now what about the waxing?

I don't suppose there is any more-discussed issue in the sport than waxing. It seems to come down to equal parts knowledge, instinct, application technique, and magic.

In the Sierra Nevadas in the 1850s, when mining camps placed heavy wagers of gold dust on miners who would represent them in ski races, the contest often came down to the "doper." He was the ski preparer. In utter secrecy the night before the race, he would mix up his special potion of beeswax, paraffin, and whatever other hopefully charmed ingredients he could think of to apply to the ski bottoms. So much money rode on these races that the doper was regarded as something like the witch doctor who could conjure up just the right spell to make the bottoms of a pair of skis fast.

I am not sure anyone really knows how wax works, though I have listened to many hours of theory. The most cogent primer I recall was that of Jack Turner, a member of the U.S. Ski Team, who at breakfast one morning explained as he diagrammed on his napkin, the following:

Crystals of snow come hard-edged, as in a new snowfall in cold weather, or smooth-sided, as in snow that has thawed and refrozen a few times.

The wax of the day must be sufficiently soft so the crystals of snow will penetrate enough to give the ski its grip but not penetrate so completely that snow will stick to the ski. If the wax you choose for the day is too hard, there will be so little penetration of crystals into the wax that the ski will slip backward when you try to push off on it. Sometimes, good ski technique can get around this tendency, if the problem isn't too extreme. But in the opposite case, the wax is so soft, and the penetration of snow crystals so extreme, the skier will pick up great immobilizing clumps of snow on the kick zone of the ski.

Look elsewhere for a detailed explanation of ski waxing in all its nuances. There are several excellent books on the market, and many of the larger areas will even put on waxing clinics from time to time. Moreover, the more days you ski with people who know what they're about, the quicker you will learn for yourself. And, when all else fails, when you want to know the wax of the day, ask a hotshot. At every touring center I've been to, the morning air is full of discussion about the wax of the day. Listen to this talk. You'll know who the hotshots are right away.

That said, here is the Chamberlain Sometimes Sure-Fire Simpleminded Waxing Style:

Cross-country waxes are color-coded to temperature and are pretty logical about it. Cold colors—blue and green—are cold-temperature waxes, and warm colors—purples to reds—are for warmer temperatures. So you stick a thermometer in the snow and know just what to do, correct? For real arctic snow, green will be the choice (or maybe special green), blue for merely cold snow, violet for that 32-degree Fahrenheit limbo, and red for thawing snow.

Well, it's almost that simple. But not quite.

Despite the temperature, if the snow has thawed and refrozen, its crystal shape will have changed irreversibly. Yesterday's hard-edged new snow, having thawed once or twice, has now lost those hard crystal edges and become old snow with round crystals. Often, the only way to get a grip on such crystals is by using *klister*—gooey stuff that comes in tubes and is color-coded similarly to the hard waxes.

Swix is not the only wax manufacturer around, but it is certainly an identifiable standard. There is a Swix kit that comes complete with all the waxes and klisters you will need. Armed with this kit, a scraper, polishing cork, a rag or paper toweling, and a lightweight propane torch you must answer two questions: What is the temperature of the snow? Are the crystals sharp (newer) or rounded (old)?

If you're a real performance skier, you'll put a grip (softer) wax on the kick zone and a glider (harder) wax on tips and tails. But that's pretty fussy and unnecessary for most users of fiberglass skis. Most of us will put a glider wax—green is my choice—over the entire base of the ski. This seals the bottom, protects it, and is a good base over which to apply the wax of the day. In many cases this base wax is applied just at the beginning of the season. After rubbing on the wax, heat it gently with the torch, then polish it in to a slick finish. (You may also make this application with a cool iron, the same as with Alpine skis, and cork-polish.)

Over this base coat (which you probably have prepared at home) you'll then make your best guess at the wax of the day. Even the neophyte, if he has listened to those around him, can come close. Read the wax tube for temperature range, and look at your thermometer. If it's fluffy stuff, go green. If it crunches a bit, blue. If it's good packing for snowballs, purple. If it's mashed potatoes, red. And if you're very, very lucky, you can skip the klister; at any rate, start without it.

ALSO KEEP IN MIND:

. . . As a general rule, go with the colder wax. Snow temperature is generally far behind the temperature of a warming day, and the penalty for being too cold is not so great as the other way around. Wax too warm, and you'll be planted like a statue. Also, you can apply warm wax over cold, and klister over hard wax, but it is almost impossible to do the reverse.

. . . We New Englanders must also watch humidity. On very humid days, it often pays to wax warmer than the temperature indicates.

. . . If you're on prepared tracks, you can wax warmer, get more kick without paying the price of clinging clumps. But in unbroken snow, when bushwhacking woods and mountain terrain, wax colder.

You are supposed to do all this waxing in a warm room—either at home or in a waxing room at a touring center—with the skis at room temperature. But I've seen plenty of top-flight ski racers sitting on the bumpers of their cars waxing before a race. Skiers often must wax while underway on the trail, too.

Most fiberglass skis have well-marked kick zones, but a rule of thumb is to wax from about 1 foot in front of the bindings to 1 foot behind. Rub the wax on side to side in overlapping smears. Then take your cork and rub it over the wax fast enough to let friction soften it to a nice polish. Repeat this waxing procedure twice, and you're set for the day, unless you must rewax for changing conditions.

Suppose you've blown it? You get out on the trail, and you've got big balls of snow under your feet? And everyone says you can't wax down in color?

Here is where you'll learn fast that, like fly fishing and choosing the right pattern for a salmon stream, no rules are cast in concrete about ski waxing. Get out the scraper and do the best you can to get the wrong wax off, then try to smear the colder wax on. If it doesn't work, daub some cold klister over the whole mess and see if that helps.

There are difficult days for waxing, when the temperature is right around freezing. The best rule I have discovered about these days is to stay on flat terrain. Remember, the worst that can happen is you'll end up walking back to Bloody Mary hour with the skis on your shoulder.

SKATING

The big development of the last decade in the sport has been skating. While Alpine skiers are very familiar with this form of propulsion across flats, the move was not common in cross-country skiing until Bill Koch introduced it in the highest levels of competition in the seventies and went on to win the Nordic World Cup. Swedish great Gunde Svan was next to pick up the technique and develop it until virtually all serious skiers had to skate to keep up.

Both in racing and recreational skiing, skating has been a most controversial development. So horrified were the European traditionalists that they tried to ban skating from top competition and only grudgingly came to accept it. Likewise, ski-touring centers, at first taking a dim view of the technique that carved up their parallel tracks, have been forced to accommodate the growing popularity of skating.

Basically, the skating technique allows the skier to set one ski at a diagonal to the track and thrust off its inside edge, then repeat the move with the alternate ski. What racers found is that skating requires less energy and produces as much as 30 percent more speed than the traditional diagonal stride.

Skating skis are shorter, the poles are longer, and there is no need for grip wax or scales in the kick zone. Some instruction is usually required to pick up the knack. Many areas reviewed in this book have made the transition to skating; some offer separate trails, while others maintain one side of a trail in single trackset, and groom the other side for skating.

THE SHORTY SKI "REVOLUTION"

The emergence of shorty skis is an idea whose time really came and went in Alpine skiing a long time ago. Basically, the point of short skis is to give skiers maximum maneuverability by chopping off the long extension of wood or plastic fore and aft of the foot itself. Thus, less to turn and get tangled up in.

Until the emergence of super-strong, space-age plastics, a ski had to be long, with enough camber to load up the stride zone and

still let the ski glide. Thus, the longer the wooden ski, the better it performed. Newer skiers had to wrestle with the awkward feel of big sticks on their feet tripping them, the first impediment to enjoying the sport.

The short skis—about 150 centimeters as opposed to a typical 210-centimeter ski—cut down that size, and the rigidity was created with the newer, stiffer, but lighter, building materials. This is particularly important when skiing downhill in tight-turning trails, when "grab-a-bush-as-you-go-by" is one of the leading techniques for making a turn. Short skis are easier to weight into a turn, and to do those quick steps from rut to rut as you change direction.

Is there a downside to shorty skis? Yes. I tried them one morning last year up at the Bretton Woods trails. They felt okay as we strided out across the flats, but soon I found that while they could kick me forward all right when it came to the glide, these skis simply didn't give me the smooth stroke ahead that my own skis did. A shortened stroke made the rhythm seem choppier than what I am used to, or enjoy.

Again, downhill on short skis, while they do maneuver with quick responses to your weighting and foot movement, once you get some speed on, they feel light and less stable than longer skis—the old Volkswagen and Cadillac comparison.

By all means, do try short skis. Even if you own some traditional long skis, if you have an opportunity to borrow or rent some shorties for a few hours, make up your own mind. My overall assessment is that, while they are not exactly a gimmick in the sport, short skis are less revolutionary than their billing suggests, and that there are serious compensations for giving up traditional length skis.

WHAT TO WEAR

Dressing for cross-country is a difficult but solvable problem. The key is layers.

Layers of thin clothing can be taken off as the skier heats up, then put back on when he stops pumping and begins to cool down. A typical outfit for a typical day: polypropylene underwear (use nothing else), wind pants below, a light jersey, loose shirt, light sweater, and a nylon shell. Although knickers and Nordic snowflake stockings look natty at the touring center, wear nylon gaiters in the backcountry. These, in effect, extend the waterproof seal of your ski boots nearly up to the knees.

There are all kinds of clothing variations, of course, and if you're really trekking in backcountry, you'll want to pack clothing in which you could survive a winter night.

This goes for the minimal tools, too: screwdriver and duct tape, wax, sunglasses, lip balm, matches, a compass, topographic maps, and any other miscellany you may need on the trail. But keep it simple. Camping stoves and elaborate waxing kits are examples of the unnecessary for me. They don't feel heavy until the tenth mile or so.

CONNECTICUT

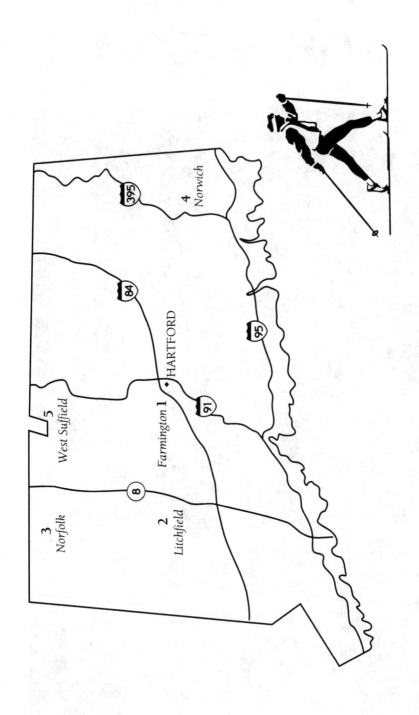

CONNECTICUT

Numbers on map refer to towns numbered below

WINDING TRAILS SKI TOURING CENTER
Off Route 4
Farmington, Connecticut 06032
(860) 677–8458

HOURS: 9:00 A.M. to 4:30 P.M.

TRAIL SYSTEM: 26 kilometers (about 15 miles)

TRAIL DIFFICULTY: Easiest, more difficult

TRAIL GROOMING: Machine groomed (about 20 kilometers) with the rest skier-tracked

RENTAL EQUIPMENT: About 200 sets

INSTRUCTION: Group and private

FOOD FACILITIES: Snack bar

LODGING: Several inns and motels in the area

HOW TO GET THERE: I–84 to Exit 39, then 1 mile west of Farmington Center to the Winding Trails Farm

Winding Trails is a 400-acre touring center set in the picturesque hills of Connecticut countryside. The entire trail system—a relatively gentle series of loops over open pasture and wooded roads—is groomed carefully and trackset for smooth, fast skiing. This is an excellent course for the runners of the sport. The center itself has a well-stocked rental shop and places heavy emphasis on its instructional program. Winding Trails is open December through March, during which it throws six nightly wine-and-cheese parties after a moonlight ski tour. In mid-January the center stages its annual Citizen's Race.

THE WHITE MEMORIAL FOUNDATION
Route 202; Box 368
Litchfield, Connecticut 06759
(860) 567–0857

HOURS: Tuesday through Saturday, 8:30 A.M. to 4:30 P.M.; Sunday, 2:00 P.M. to 5:00 P.M.

TRAIL SYSTEM: 48 kilometers (30 miles)

TRAIL DIFFICULTY: Easiest, more difficult, most difficult

TRAIL GROOMING: None

RENTAL EQUIPMENT: No

INSTRUCTION: No

FOOD FACILITIES: In Litchfield

LODGING: Inns and motels in the area

HOW TO GET THERE: From Hartford, Route 202 heading west through Litchfield for 2½ miles to a left turn at the White Memorial sign

The White Memorial Foundation is a lovely 4,000-acre sanctuary dedicated to conservation, education, recreation, and nature research. The terrain, with its crisscrossing carriage roads and trails, is still in its uninterrupted natural state; no motor vehicles are allowed anywhere on the property. The skiing is of the primitive, bushwhacking variety, though tracks are generally cut by previous skiers. The countryside is not especially challenging, except to runners, though one or two real twisters can be found if one really wants to find them. The trail loops through woods down to the shores of Bantam Lake. There is no trail fee here, though maps may be purchased at the museum for about $1.00 A warming-waxing-picnicking facility is also available.

MAPLEWOOD FARM

129 Grantville Road
Norfolk, Connecticut 06058
(860) 542–5882

HOURS: 9:00 A.M. to dusk

TRAIL SYSTEM: 8 kilometers (about 5 miles) plus 400 acres of open meadow and woodland skiing

TRAIL DIFFICULTY: Mostly intermediate

TRAIL GROOMING: About 8 kilometers groomed and tracked

RENTAL EQUIPMENT: Yes

INSTRUCTION: By appointment

FOOD FACILITIES: Snacks and refreshments

LODGING: Motels and inns in the area

HOW TO GET THERE: Follow the Massachusetts Turnpike to Exit 35 in Stockbridge, then Route 7 heading north to Caanan, then head east on Route 44 to Norfolk. From Norfolk Center, follow Route 272 south 1 7/10 miles to Winchester Road, then take the first left onto Grantville Road. Maplewood Farm is 1 mile on the left.

Set in the southern Berkshires, Maplewood Farm is a year-round nature center set on a 400-acre New England farm that dates back to the last century. It is rustic in its setting of the rolling hill country, and bikers enjoy the region in the summer as much as skiers do in the winter. Most skiing is open meadow, which makes it a good place to learn the sport. More extensive trails wind through the woods with openings that overlook the river and many ponds in the area. This is very much an area for skiers who place a premium on the charm of their setting and like lots of low-stress, classic-style touring.

QUINEBAUG VALLEY SKI TOURING CENTER

Roosevelt Avenue, Box 29
Norwich, Connecticut 06360
(860) 886–2284

HOURS: 9:00 A.M. to 4:00 P.M.

TRAIL SYSTEM: 11 kilometers (about 7 miles)

TRAIL DIFFICULTY: Easiest, more difficult, most difficult

TRAIL GROOMING: Packed but not trackset

RENTAL EQUIPMENT: 100 sets

INSTRUCTION: PSIA-certified instructor on weekends

FOOD FACILITIES: Snack bar at the center

LODGING: Hotels, inns, and motels within 3 miles

HOW TO GET THERE: Connecticut Turnpike to Route 12 in Norwich,
   follow signs

This active dairy farm features that most pleasant sort of open-field skiing that lets the inexperienced skier practice in a low-stress environment but also allows runners to really work out over tracks well set by previous skiers. From the open fields—cow pastures—skiers can access the nearby woodlands that glance in and out of open pastures. This is fine touring when the snow is available. Norwich is a good-sized town just 3 miles from the touring center and has an entire range of rentals, retail, food, and lodging.

CEDAR BROOK FARMS CROSS-COUNTRY SKI CENTER

1481 Ratley Road
West Suffield, Connecticut 06093
(860) 668–5026

HOURS: 9:00 A.M. to dusk

TRAIL SYSTEM: 10 kilometers (6 2/10 miles)

TRAIL DIFFICULTY: Easiest, more difficult

TRAIL GROOMING: Groomed and trackset daily

RENTAL EQUIPMENT: More than 100 sets

INSTRUCTION: Yes

FOOD FACILITIES: Small snack bar for soups and sandwiches

LODGING: In the area, within 8 miles

HOW TO GET THERE: Massachusetts Turnpike to I–91 heading south to Route 57. Take Route 57 through Feeding Hills to Southwest Street, which changes its name to Ratley Road as you enter Connecticut.

When the snow is right, this 200-acre touring center offers all the delights of skiing on a real working New England Morgan Horse farm with pastureland, woods, ponds, and streams well within the reach of all skiers. Animals (safely confined) watch as you pass through the pasture. From this open skiing, the trails course through a very pretty woodland area, then bring skiers back into the pasture. This can be hard-run ski touring or pleasant, gentle cruising, as you wish. There's a warming hut on the property as skiers cross over from a loop through Enchanted Forest and back through Cornstalk Patch and Scarecrow Hill. Fanciful names, delightful skiing.

MASSACHUSETTS

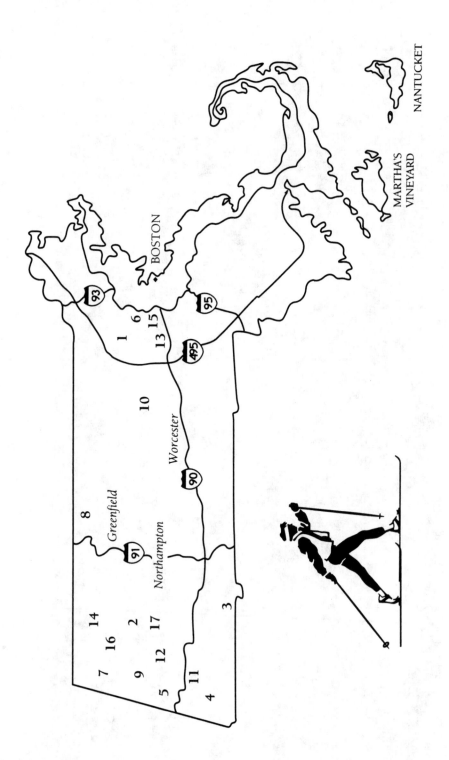

BOSTON

NANTUCKET

MARTHA'S
VINEYARD

93

95

495

6 15

1

13

10

Worcester

90

Greenfield

8

91

Northampton

14

7 16

2

9 12 17

5

11

3

4

MASSACHUSETTS

Numbers on map refer to towns numbered below

GREAT BROOK FARM SKI TOURING CENTER
1018 Lowell Street
Carlisle, Massachusetts 01741-0720
(508) 369–7486

HOURS: 9:00 A.M. to 4:30 P.M.; Tuesday and Thursday, 9:00 A.M. to 9:00 P.M.

TRAIL SYSTEM: 15 kilometers (about 9 miles)

TRAIL DIFFICULTY: Easiest, more difficult, most difficult

TRAIL GROOMING: Groomed and double trackset

RENTAL EQUIPMENT: Yes

INSTRUCTION: Certified professional ski school

FOOD FACILITIES: Snacks, hot cider, coffee, tea

LODGING: None

HOW TO GET THERE: I–495 to Route 4 in Chelmsford; right on Route 4 and follow to Lowell Road

Just forty minutes from Boston, Great Brook Farm is a fine and complete daytrip ski center with its 15-kilometer trail system winding over farm meadows, though deep woodlands, and over frozen ponds. Like the Weston Track, Great Brook is one of very few areas that offers snow making over a 1-kilometer loop. Night skiing is also available over a 1½-kilometer loop.

Great Brook caters to organized race programs and youth groups and puts on a citizen race every Tuesday night. There is an organized Bill Koch League for grade-schoolers.

The area is perfect for Boston-area recreational skiers looking for regular exercise or to get in shape for upcountry.

SWIFT RIVER INN

151 South Street
Cummington, Massachusetts 01026
(413) 634–5751

HOURS: 9:00 A.M. to 5:00 P.M.; Thursday through Saturday evenings, 6:30 to 9:30 P.M.

TRAIL SYSTEM: 20 kilometers (about 13 miles) with 1½ kilometers (about 1 mile) lighted for night skiing

TRAIL DIFFICULTY: Easiest, more difficult, most difficult

TRAIL GROOMING: As needed. Groomed and tracked with some skating

RENTAL EQUIPMENT: Yes

INSTRUCTION: PSIA-certified school

FOOD FACILITIES: Restaurant at resort

LODGING: Inn offers 21 rooms in turn-of-the-century style

HOW TO GET THERE: Route 91 heading north to Northampton; Route 9 heading west to Cummington (26 miles); turn right into town and follow signs

Swift River, at 1,250 feet in the Berkshire uplands, is the largest and among the most popular ski-touring areas in southern New England. With good elevation despite the southerly location, the skiing usually remains long into the spring.

The well-marked and well-groomed trail system is spread out over 560 acres of rolling foothills that take skiers through the hardwood forests of the wild turkey and over dazzling white meadowland. The trail difficulty is geared toward novice and intermediate skiers with a nice, leisurely "low-stress" feel about the place.

The accommodations include a wonderfully big restaurant and a well-appointed Nordic retail store.

MAPLE CORNER FARM CROSS-COUNTRY SKI AREA

Beech Hill Road
Granville, Massachusetts 01034
(413) 357–8829

HOURS: 9:00 A.M. to 5:00 P.M.

TRAIL SYSTEM: More than 20 kilometers (about 12 miles) of marked trails; 15 kilometers groomed; access to a 500-acre tract of wilderness skiing

TRAIL DIFFICULTY: Easiest, more difficult, most difficult

TRAIL GROOMING: Groomed and trackset

RENTAL EQUIPMENT: Yes

INSTRUCTION: Yes

FOOD FACILITIES: Snack bar at the area and a skiers' lounge with open fireplace

LODGING: Available in the area. Call the main number at the farm for listings

HOW TO GET THERE: From the Springfield area follow Route 20 heading west to Route 23 to Blandford. Stay on route 23 through Blandford Center and down the hill to Beech Hill Road on the left. Follow Beech Hill past the Granville town line. The ski center is 1/2 mile into Granville, on the left.

Maple Corner Farm Cross-Country Ski Area is located in the Berkshire foothills near the historic General Knox Trail. The ski area is an authentic family farm that has been in continuous operation since 1840. Once a working dairy and beef operation, the farm now raises hay and makes maple syrup and other maple products; visitors can watch the maple sap boiling in the sugar house.

The trails lead skiers through gentle rolling pastures and large meadows, along mountain streams and beaver ponds. One trail runs through the current sugar bush, which includes old sugaring sites of bygone years, then into the hemlock forest beyond. This is one of the lovelier offerings in the Berkshires, and the trails are wonderfully groomed for serious running, if that is your preference. Wilderness skiers have a virtually infinite area of open meadows and woodlands for simple meandering. Sandwiches, homemade soups, hot chocolate, and cider are served around the open fireplace after the day's skiing.

BUTTERNUT SKI TOURING

Route 23 (Butternut Ski Area Access Road)
Great Barrington, Massachusetts 01230
(413) 528–0610

HOURS: 9:00 A.M. to 4:00 P.M. Thursday through Sunday and school vacation weeks

TRAIL SYSTEM: 8 kilometers (about 5 miles) of tracks, plus open field skiing; no skating

TRAIL DIFFICULTY: Easiest, more difficult

TRAIL GROOMING: Daily

RENTAL EQUIPMENT: 100 sets

INSTRUCTION: PSIA-certified; group and private lessons

FOOD FACILITIES: Cafeteria at the Butternut Ski Area

LODGING: Inns, motels, and guest houses in the area

HOW TO GET THERE: I–90 to Exit 2 at Lee, Massachusetts; Route 102 heading west to Route 7 heading south to Route 23, then east to Butternut

Like many touring areas associated with established downhill areas, Butternut Ski Touring shares the benefits of the Alpine accommodations (including the nursery for three- to six-year olds), and naturally lures the skinny skiers onto the Alpine slopes to take a shot at some Telemarking. Whether there is any truth to the old chestnut, "If you can walk, you can cross-country ski," it definitely does not apply to Telemark turning on downhill slopes. Butternut, however, is an excellent place to get lessons for this graceful move. The area has an excellent ski school that can take you to the downhill slopes for lessons.

Spreading out from the warming hut beside a pretty pond, the touring area is a pristine piece of the Berkshire countryside whose 7 miles of gentle, well-groomed trails are near a 45-kilometer trail system in Beartown State Forest; the touring center has maps of this system.

KENNEDY PARK

Lenox, Massachusetts 01240
(413) 637–3010

HOURS: 7:00 A.M. to 4:00 P.M.

TRAIL SYSTEM: None; 600-acre park

TRAIL DIFFICULTY: Easiest, more difficult

TRAIL GROOMING: No

RENTAL EQUIPMENT: At a nearby ski shop. Call for details

INSTRUCTION: No

FOOD FACILITIES: In the Lenox area

LODGING: In the area

HOW TO GET THERE: Take Massachusetts Turnpike to Exit 2; west on
Route 7 then south to the park in Lenox

Kennedy Park is an open 600-acre recreation area used year-round
for a variety of sports. There is some gladed and wooded terrain
around the park, and the many skiers who use the land make good
tracks for those who do not like breaking trail. While there are no
facilities at the park itself, this Berkshire town offers all services,
from food to rentals and retail facilities.

LINCOLN GUIDE SERVICE

Lincoln Road
Lincoln, Massachusetts 01773
(617) 259–9204

HOURS: Monday through Wednesday 9:00 A.M. to 6:00 P.M.; Thursday and Friday 9:00 A.M. to 8:00 P.M.; Saturday and Sunday
9:00 A.M. to 5:00 P.M.

TRAIL SYSTEM: 20 kilometers (about 13 miles)

TRAIL DIFFICULTY: Easiest, more difficult

TRAIL GROOMING: None

RENTAL EQUIPMENT: 200 sets

INSTRUCTION: PSIA-certified

FOOD FACILITIES: The nearest of three restaurants is within 50 yards of the skiing; lunches and deli counter at area.

LODGING: Motels in the area

HOW TO GET THERE: I–95 to Exit 28 (Trapelo Road); west for 2 miles; left at the Lincoln Street stop sign, then 1 mile to the center

Lincoln Guide Service is partly a retail operation that accesses town-owned conservation land and partly a dream of Mike Farny to put together a significant touring area especially convenient to people from greater Boston. The open conservation land begins at the center's back door, and a rolling, well-groomed trail system branches out through the country where Henry David Thoreau hiked and observed nature. One of the trails, in fact, leads skiers along ponds of the Sudbury River to Thoreau's beloved Walden Pond in Concord, while other trails mix challenge with relaxing cruises. All trails are well marked, and the center is well stocked with rental and retail goods.

BRODIE MOUNTAIN CROSS-COUNTRY TOURING
Route 7
New Ashford, Massachusetts 01237
(413) 443–4752

HOURS: 9:00 A.M. to 5:00 P.M.

TRAIL SYSTEM: 25 kilometers (about 16 miles)

TRAIL DIFFICULTY: Easiest, more difficult, most difficult

TRAIL GROOMING: Yes, trackset with two flat areas; skating lanes

RENTAL EQUIPMENT: Yes

INSTRUCTION: Yes

FOOD FACILITIES: The Blarney Room in the main lodge serves lunch and dinner

LODGING: Hotel at the ski area, and several facilities nearby

HOW TO GET THERE: Route 2 to Route 7; north for 9 miles beyond Pittsfield. Midway between Pittsfield and Williamstown on Route 7

This popular Berkshire-region Alpine area incorporates the advantages of snow-making and base-lodge facilities into its Nordic facility. The trail system combines about 25 kilometers of wide, groomed and trackset trails with another 40 kilometers of wilderness touring, then limitless bushwhacking out in the Mount Grey-lock Reservation. The skiing has good variety, from rolling pasture-land and open fields, to heart-pumping hills and closed, wooded roads that meander through these Berkshire foothills and past some most unusual rock formations. This is a land fecund with wildlife of all kinds. The groomed trail system was designed by former Olympic skier Bud Fischer and is used for training by the Williams College Ski Team. Tennis, racketball, and sauna are available, and several races are staged here throughout the season.

NORTHFIELD MOUNTAIN SKI TOURING CENTER
Route 63
Northfield, Massachusetts 01360
(413) 659–3713

HOURS: 9:00 A.M. to 5:00 P.M.

TRAIL SYSTEM: 40 kilometers (25 miles)

TRAIL DIFFICULTY: Easiest, more difficult, most difficult

TRAIL GROOMING: Daily

RENTAL EQUIPMENT: Yes

INSTRUCTION: PSIA-certified

FOOD FACILITIES: Chocolate Pot snack area; outdoor barbecue-pit food service at base lodge; both open on weekends and holidays only

LODGING: Several motels and inns within 5 miles of the center

HOW TO GET THERE: I–91 to Exit 27; Route 2 heading east to Route 63 heading north; 2 miles to the center

More than 40 kilometers of double tracks set daily over wide trails groomed with Alpine equipment, an active racing program, and a lineup of instructors who teach some 5,000 skiers annually make Northfield one of the largest learning centers in southern New Eng-land. The area pioneered the concept of grooming with Alpine rollers and prides itself on creating a ski surface just a little bigger and better than average.

In addition to recreational family touring, Northfield also takes pride in its Fast-Track Ski Camp for would-be racers who want to learn the sport from the likes of former U.S. Ski Team Olympian

Tim Caldwell. Hank Lange and John Tidd are also PSIA instructors.

Three well-traveled trail systems converge at The Chocolate Pot, where skiers warm themselves in front of a big fire and sip hot chocolate and soup. Other snacks are available from an outdoor barbecue pit. During the week Northfield Mountain offers instruction and rentals for elementary-school-agers. Six miles of trails are reserved for snowshoers.

CANOE MEADOWS WILDLIFE SANCTUARY

Holmes Road
Pittsfield, Massachusetts 01201
(413) 637–0320

HOURS: 9:00 A.M. to 4:00 P.M., weekends only

TRAIL SYSTEM: 5 kilometers (about 3 miles)

TRAIL DIFFICULTY: Easiest

TRAIL GROOMING: No

RENTAL EQUIPMENT: None at facility. Ski shop nearby, in Lenox

INSTRUCTION: Saturday clinics by appointment

FOOD FACILITIES: None at ski area, but restaurants nearby

LODGING: Motels and inns in area

HOW TO GET THERE: Massachusetts Turnpike to Exit 2 at Lee; Route 7 to Holmes Road. Turn right and drive for 2 miles to entrance of Canoe Meadows Wildlife Sanctuary.

Canoe Meadows is a Massachusetts Audubon Society sanctuary comprising 260 wooded acres bordered by the Housatonic River. It is not so much a ski facility as simply a lovely piece of wild land open for weekend ski touring. There are wildlife tours of the property by appointment. Outhouses are available on the site.

WACHUSETT MOUNTAIN SKI AREA

Mountain Road
Princeton, Massachusetts 01541
(508) 464–2788

HOURS: Weekdays 9:00 A.M. to dusk; Saturday, Sunday, and holidays, 8:00 A.M. to dusk

TRAIL SYSTEM: 19 kilometers (about 11 miles)

TRAIL DIFFICULTY: Easiest, more difficult, most difficult

TRAIL GROOMING: Groomed and trackset, as needed

RENTAL EQUIPMENT: Yes

INSTRUCTION: 10:30 A.M. to 1:00 P.M., or by appointment. Telemark. PSIA instructors

FOOD FACILITIES: Full cafeteria with lounge and ice-cream shop

LODGING: Several hotels and motels within a fifteen-minute drive

HOW TO GET THERE: Route 2 heading west to Route 140 heading south. The area is 3½ miles from the exit.

Close to Boston, Wachusett is another of those touring areas that brings the amenities of the downhill area and the challenge to cross-country skiers to try their hand—and feet—at Telemarking down Alpine slopes. Instruction is necessary for this, and it is available. The area's 19 kilometers of groomed and trackset trails wind over the top of Wachusettt's 2,000-foot elevation and offer skiers a nice view of what Native Americans named "the great hill." The cross-country trails are wide and well maintained, and the terrain has some spicy variety for all levels of skiers. Maps, rentals, instruction, and full base-lodge facilities.

OAK N' SPRUCE RESORT

South Lee, Massachusetts 01260
(413) 243–3500

HOURS: Dawn to dusk

TRAIL SYSTEM: 10 mile loop; novice area; 50 kilometers (about 30

miles) of trails in the adjoining state forest, open to the public

TRAIL DIFFICULTY: Easiest, more difficult

TRAIL GROOMING: On the 2-mile novice loop

RENTAL EQUIPMENT: 100 sets

INSTRUCTION: Yes

FOOD FACILITIES: Continental-style restaurant; hot drinks and snacks at center

LODGING: 150 units (condos and hotel rooms) at the resort

HOW TO GET THERE: Massachusetts Turnpike to Exit 2 in Lee; Route 102 heading west to Oak n' Spruce

This touring center has 300 acres of open fields and a groomed, trackset 2-mile loop. But after warming up here, skiers plunge into the 12,000-acre Beartown State Forest and follow the unplowed country roads, forest trails, and open-meadow touring. This is the pristine land of the whitetailed deer and wild turkey.

For beginners or serious touring skiers, Oak n' Spruce accommodates all levels. Aside from planned group activities—snowshoeing, skating, and tobogganing—the area has plenty of health club-pool-sauna-Jacuzzi-cocktail lounge activity for the indoor sports enthusiast.

BUCKSTEEP MANOR CROSS-COUNTRY SKI CENTER

Washington Mountain Road
Washington, Massachusetts 01223
(413) 623–5535

HOURS: 8:00 A.M. to 4:30 P.M.

TRAIL SYSTEM: 25 kilometers (about 16 miles)

TRAIL DIFFICULTY: Easiest, more difficult, most difficult

TRAIL GROOMING: Machine trackset, as needed; some skating lanes

RENTAL EQUIPMENT: 100 sets; retail shop

INSTRUCTION: Private and group, by appointment

FOOD FACILITIES: Manor Kitchen Restaurant on premises serves meals weekends and holidays. Skier Sunday Brunch special; lunch all week

LODGING: Manor Inn, call (413) 623–5535

HOW TO GET THERE: I–90 to Exit 2 at Lee; Route 20 heading east, then Route 8 heading north to Washington

High atop the Berkshire Hills between October and Washington peaks, Bucksteep Manor's 1,900-foot elevation ensures one of the longest ski seasons in the region. The nicely groomed trails wind through snow-covered fir thickets, stream beds, and bogs, and across pristine white meadows that overlook mountain valleys. Skiers can also incorporate on their tour the trail system of nearby October Mountain.

As picturesque as the land is the Manor Inn itself, a Victorian estate that serves fine homemade food in front of a big wood fire. Here are nightly entertainment and moonlight tours. Bucksteep offers citizen racing and guided tours of the Appalachian Trail. Sleigh rides in the state forest are also offered.

CROSS-COUNTRY SKIING AND SNOWSHOEING IN WAYLAND

Conservation Commission
Wayland, Massachusetts 01778
(508) 358–7701 weekdays

HOW TO GET THERE: I–95 to Route 20 to Wayland

Although Wayland is not the only community to open large tracts of public land to skiing and snowshoeing, it is one of the best, certainly considering how close it is to the large metropolitan area of greater Boston. The Conservation Commission makes no special effort to groom or trackset—or even to clear fallen brush from the trails. Yet the woodland trails, which web throughout almost 600 acres of woods and open meadows, are often traced by skiers very soon after a new snowfall. There are four areas: Heard Farm, Cow Common, Upper Mill Brook, and Mainstone Area. Heard Farm is the best skiing area. The parcel consists of a scenic farm with rolling meadows and woods full of wildlife. It is accessible from a parking lot off the end of Heard Road. Cow Common, close to the original

Sudbury village, is similar to Heard Farm but somewhat flatter. It has parking off Route 27. Upper Mill Brook is entirely wooded, and the skiing is tougher by far. Mainstone has lots of trails, but the equestrians often ride the snow off them early in the day. The trustees do keep the trails marked and graded—a good thing since there are some really tough descents that one should know about beforehand. They also provide a map of the entire area. Happily, no motorized vehicles are allowed in Wayland's conservation.

STUMP SPROUTS

West Hill Road
West Hawley, Massachusetts 01339
(413) 339-4265

HOURS: 9:00 A.M. to sunset, weekends and vacation weeks; on weekdays call ahead

TRAIL SYSTEM: 25 kilometers (about 15 miles)

TRAIL DIFFICULTY: Easiest to most difficult; mostly intermediate

TRAIL GROOMING: 20 kilometers groomed in classical skiing, with about 5 kilometers groomed for skating

RENTAL EQUIPMENT: 50 sets

INSTRUCTION: At 10:00 A.M. daily, or by appointment

FOOD FACILITIES: The guest lodge serves three meals daily, and snacks and soups are available at the center

LODGING: 10 rooms at the center, with motels nearby

HOW TO GET THERE: From Boston, follow Route 2 to Charlemont, Massachusetts, then go south 6 miles on Route 8A. Turn right up West Hill Road.

Stump Sprouts is a wilderness area both nestled in the Berkshire foothills and trekking up to a mountain summit where skiers enjoy the lovely overview of the western Massachusetts hills. Carved out of the deep woodlands, most of the area's trails are narrow, single-tracked, built for minimum impact on the countryside. Four of the trails converge at High Lookout on Lone Boulder Hill, a 2,000-foot highland lookout over the countryside. A newly cut glades trail descends from Lone Boulder Hill, featuring ungroomed Telemark ski-

ing. There is also an "interpretive" trail in which skiers match their skiing to the terrain features. Stump Sprouts has a definite old-world feel to it both on the trails and in the dining room and inn. Skiers should bring their own bedding.

WESTON SKI TRACK

At the Leo J. Martin Golf Course
Box 426, Park Road
Weston, Massachusetts 02166
(617) 891–6575

HOURS: Monday through Saturday 9:00 A.M. to 10:00 P.M.; Sunday 9:00 A.M. to 6:00 P.M.

TRAIL SYSTEM: 15 kilometers (about 9 miles)

TRAIL DIFFICULTY: Easiest, more difficult

TRAIL GROOMING: Trackset daily; skating lanes

RENTAL EQUIPMENT: Yes

INSTRUCTION: PSIA-certified

FOOD FACILITIES: Cafe and snack bar on premises

LODGING: Many hotels and motels in the area

HOW TO GET THERE: I–90 to Exit 15, onto I–95 to exit 25; north to Route 30, then west to a left turn onto Park Road and to Weston Ski Track

As cross-country skiing caught on among Bostonians during the last two decades, a need arose for local areas near the city. Mike Farny and The Lincoln Guide Service, given a shove by M. R. Montgomery of the *Boston Globe,* opened the Weston Track on a popular MDC golf course. Since those origins in the early 1970s, the area has grown as a place to work out, to get excellent lessons, and to practice for trips upcountry.

And lest ye think Weston sounds rather small and insignificant, you'll encounter some of the serious folks in the sport here, wearing their one-piece body suits and zinging around the loops at 15 miles an hour. Here high school and college teams work out over the carefully groomed tracks. The addition of snow making makes it possible to ski here even when there's no snow in the flatlands. After a workout, skiers relax in the Langlaufer Cafe, whose name translates: "Cross-country skiers live longer." There are showers, lockers, waxing areas, and a full retail shop. It goes without saying that there are plenty of citizen races at the track, as well as clinics on everything from waxing to skating technique.

NOTCHVIEW RESERVATION

83 Old Route 9
Windsor, Massachusetts 01270
(413) 684–0148

HOURS: Dawn to dusk from December 1 through March 1

TRAIL SYSTEM: 25 kilometers (about 16 miles); 3,000-acre reservation

TRAIL DIFFICULTY: Easiest, more difficult, and most difficult

TRAIL GROOMING: 15 kilometers

RENTAL EQUIPMENT: No

INSTRUCTION: None

FOOD FACILITIES: Picnic room, and several restaurants within 5 miles

LODGING: Several motels and inns within 5 miles in Windsor and Stockbridge

HOW TO GET THERE: Massachusetts Turnpike to Lee; Route 7 heading north to Pittsfield, Massachusetts; then Route 9 heading east for about 14 miles to Notchview

Many knowledgeable cross-country aficionados consider Notchview one of the best wilderness ski areas in the Berkshires, with its 25-kilometer spider web of trails for every level of skiing challenge. Main loops plunge along through this spruce forest so appreciated by small game, deer, and a growing flock of wild turkeys. Ancient stone walls and cellar holes poignantly bespeak a rugged farming history. Part of the Hoosac Range, Notchview Reservation has a system of trails running over old fire and logging roads, with clear difficulty-level signs at each intersection, all at a mile-high elevation.

The main loop, Circuit Trail, leads to a pasture with a sudden vista of the notch, cut by Shaw Brook, a tributary of the Westfield River. It is this view that gives the area its name. A most challenging trail is a steep climb up Judges Hill, rising to 2,300 feet, the highest point in Windsor. The snow comes early here and hangs in late because of the spruce shade. Budds Visitors Center is on the premises with rest rooms, a picnic room with a big fireplace, and a waxing room. Notchview is one of sixty-nine properties owned by the Trustees of Reservations, a private, nonprofit organization founded in 1891 to preserve beautiful and historic places in Massachusetts.

HICKORY HILL TOURING CENTER

Box 39
Buffington Hill Road
Worthington, Massachusetts 01098
(413) 238–5813

HOURS: 9:00 A.M. to dusk

TRAIL SYSTEM: 25 kilometers (about 15 miles)

TRAIL DIFFICULTY: Easiest, more difficult, most difficult

TRAIL GROOMING: Machine double trackset

RENTAL EQUIPMENT: 250 sets

INSTRUCTION: Yes

FOOD FACILITIES: Food service in the barn on weekends; cocktails and meals

LODGING: Inns and motels in the area within 20 miles; bed-and-breakfast nearby

HOW TO GET THERE: I–91 to Northampton; Route 9 heading northwest to Route 143; west on Route 112 and Worthington, then right onto Buffington Hill Road

With an expanded trail system, good elevation (1,800 feet) to ensure long seasons, and improvements each year, Hickory Hill is developing as a popular ski center in the Berkshires.

The 25 kilometers of groomed, trackset, and well-marked trails are spread out over 700 acres of old New England farm country and adjoining hardwood forests. The rolling meadowland is interlaced with old colonial stone walls, and in spots skiers are treated to lovely overlooks of 40 miles and more out toward New York State. Hickory Hill offers a special package for beginners. Maps and trail guides are available. The barn serves beverages, baked goods, and a soup du jour in front of a constantly roaring fireplace. There is a fulsome schedule of moonlight and maple-sugar tours, as well as an old-fashioned pig roast in mid-season. The high elevation usually ensures excellent snow cover.

VERMONT

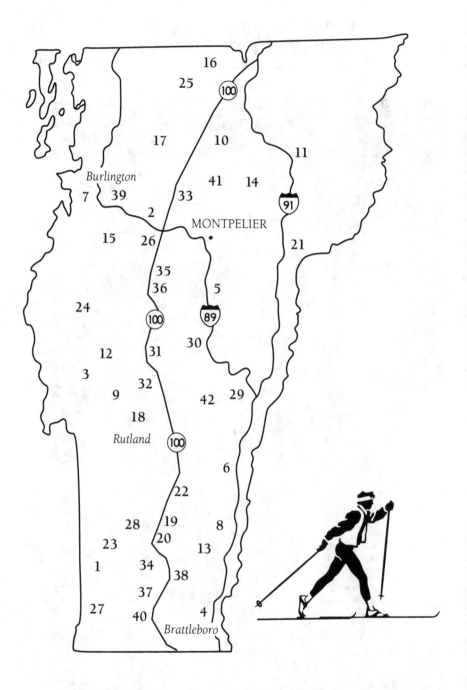

VERMONT

Numbers on map refer to towns numbered below

THE WEST MOUNTAIN INN

Route 313, River Road
Arlington, Vermont 05250
(802) 375–6516

HOURS: Daylight

TRAIL SYSTEM: 9 kilometers (about 5 miles)

TRAIL DIFFICULTY: Easiest, more difficult, most difficult

TRAIL GROOMING: None; wilderness trails

RENTAL EQUIPMENT: None

INSTRUCTION: None

FOOD FACILITIES: Breakfast, 8:00 A.M. to 10:00 A.M.; dinner 7:00 P.M.,
by reservation only

LODGING: Eighteen rooms in three buildings at the inn

HOW TO GET THERE: Route I–91 to Brattleboro, Vermont; Route 9
heading west to Bennington; Route 7 heading north to Arlington,
then Route 313 going west to West Mountain Road, and up the hill

This wilderness area contains the best sort of Vermont inn—hidden
in the splendid intimate surroundings of the Batten Kill River woodlands. From the door of the inn, skiers look over the famous Batten
Kill with its trout-fishing lore, then begin to work off breakfast, first
on the easy flats, then on the seemingly endless ruggedness of the
old logging trails. Some of these trails can get woolly and steep, but
they are quite wide. Nearer to the inn is a wonderful all-purpose
hill for Telemark practice or moonlight tobogganing.

At night in front of the inn's huge fireplace, you'll be served as
fine cuisine as there is in Vermont, starting with hot drinks and
cocktails and followed by an artistic meal and after-dinner activity
around the piano. There are eighteen rooms, cottages, and a two-
bedroom housekeeping apartment as well.

BOLTON VALLEY CROSS-COUNTRY CENTER

Bolton Valley Ski Resort
Bolton, Vermont 05477
(802) 434–2131

HOURS: 9:00 A.M. to 4:00 P.M.

TRAIL SYSTEM: More than 100 kilometers (about 60 miles)

TRAIL DIFFICULTY: Easiest, more difficult, most difficult

TRAIL GROOMING: 10 kilometers rolled and trackset; 20 kilometers rolled; remainder, wilderness skiing

RENTAL EQUIPMENT: Yes

INSTRUCTION: Beginning group to private Telemark

FOOD FACILITIES: Eight separate dining experiences

LODGING: Bolton Valley Lodge has an eighty-five-bed capacity; other motels and inns in the area

HOW TO GET THERE: I–95 to I–89 to Exit 10; Route 2 and Bolton access road to the ski area

Bolton Valley's gentle Alpine slopes work to the ski tourer's advantage. The area has a very well developed Nordic trail system set into the 2,100-foot elevation, and that means snow—lots of it—well into April most years. But take advantage of Bolton's downhill capability, and you will become an expert Telemarker as well. Skiers begin with the Sitzmark Trail, graduate to the intermediate Telemark trail, then try Cliffhanger, where the trail system works into the Trapp Family Lodge and Mt. Mansfield—a trek for experts. Skiers taking this route or any other may take the group lessons available at Bolton Valley beginning at 10:00 A.M. Aside from a full-complement retail and rental shop, Bolton Valley has all the amenities of a major downhill ski area, and cross-country tourers are welcome as well.

CHURCHILL HOUSE INN AND CROSS-COUNTRY SKI CENTER

Route 73
Brandon, Vermont 05733
(802) 247-3300

HOURS: 10:00 A.M. to 4:00 P.M.

TRAIL SYSTEM: 25 kilometers (15 miles)

TRAIL DIFFICULTY: Easiest, more difficult, most difficult

TRAIL GROOMING: 20 kilometers groomed and trackset daily

RENTAL EQUIPMENT: No

INSTRUCTION: Yes

FOOD FACILITIES: Dining for guests; other restaurants within 5 miles

LODGING: Nine rooms at the inn with many hotels and motels in the area

HOW TO GET THERE: I-91 to I-89 heading west; to exit 3; west on Route 107 to 100 north to Route 73 west; 13 miles on 73 going west

Churchill House is part of a three-lodge, four-day inn-to-inn trip from north to south that lets skiers get some real miles under the boards traveling from Bristol to Chittenden. Churchill is a stout, three-story farmhouse of the Civil War period and preserves the century-old feel inside and out. The trail system begins with groomed and trackset loops of flattish terrain near the inn, then flowers out into some rugged wilderness challenge. Along several of the trail systems, skiers get sudden vistas of the Adirondacks. The system winds into the Green Mountain National Forest and its nearly limitless skiing. Back at the inn, with its full fare of cocktails and gourmet dining, skiers find rentals and retail available, guided tours, and organized events. In the waxing hut, hot soup and bread are always available to see one through to the inn's sumptuous meals.

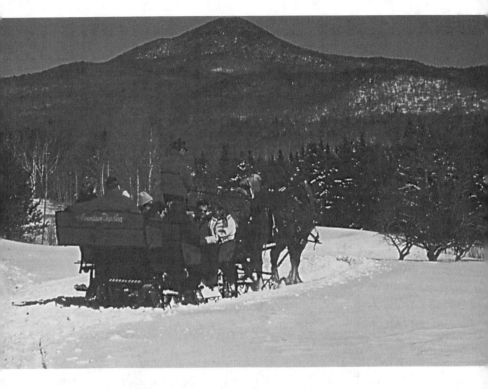

BRATTLEBORO OUTING CLUB SKI HUT
Box 335, Upper Drummerston Road
Brattleboro, Vermont 05301
(802) 254–4081 or (802) 254–4712

HOURS: 9:00 A.M. to 4:00 P.M.

TRAIL SYSTEM: 15 kilometers (about 9 miles)

TRAIL DIFFICULTY: Easiest, more difficult

TRAIL GROOMING: All trails packed for skating and trackset

RENTAL EQUIPMENT: Yes

INSTRUCTION: By appointment

FOOD FACILITIES: 2 miles away in Brattleboro

LODGING: In Brattleboro

HOW TO GET THERE: I–93 to Brattleboro to second exit; Route 30 to
Upper Dummerston Road to the Outing Club

This wide-open ski area is spread out across a nine-hole golf course and the nearby woodlands. The trails are groomed and used often by the more athletic of the cross-country fraternity. Some trails cross bridges and skirt ponds; others are flat runners along the fairways. The system is anchored by a center with ski shop, warming hut, rentals, and snacks. Skiers here can also sign up for moonlight excursions.

GREEN TRAILS INN & SKI TOURING CENTER
Pond Village
Brookfield, Vermont 05036
(802) 276–3412 or (800) 243–3412

HOURS: 9:00 A.M. to 5:00 P.M.

TRAIL SYSTEM: 36 kilometers (about 23 miles)

TRAIL DIFFICULTY: Easiest, more difficult, most difficult

TRAIL GROOMING: Machine groomed and trackset

RENTAL EQUIPMENT: Yes

INSTRUCTION: PSIA-certified instructors by appointment at the inn

FOOD FACILITIES: Breakfast and dinner at the center's restaurant; lunches available to skiers

LODGING: Fifteen rooms at the inn

HOW TO GET THERE: I–91 to I–89, northeast to Vermont Exit 4; Route 66 heading east to Randolph Center, then north for 7½ miles to Brookfield, follow signs to the center

Green Trails Inn & Ski Touring Center is an area that keeps evolving around what was once nineteenth-century farmland in the historic village of Brookfield, Vermont. Encompassing a restored farmhouse and two other residences, the center offers fifteen nice rooms with plenty of Victorian and early American flavor. The ski-trail system keeps expanding over the rolling pastureland, frozen lakes, and hills of the region; one trail takes skiers across the famed floating bridge over a narrow pond. Skating, snowshoeing, and sleigh rides complete this winter postcard scene. The trail system itself incorporates other nearby trail systems for plenty of skiing—including the Allis State Park on 400 acres of groomed and wilderness trails. The center has complete rental and retail offerings, and the food is homemade and delicious.

ASCUTNEY MOUNTAIN RESORT TOURING CENTER

Route 44
Brownsville, Vermont 05037
(802) 484–7711 or (800) 243–0011

HOURS: Saturday, Sunday, all holidays, and vacation weeks, 8:30 A.M. to 4:00 P.M.

TRAIL SYSTEM: 32 kilometers (20 miles)

TRAIL DIFFICULTY: Easiest, more difficult, most difficult

TRAIL GROOMING: Daily

RENTAL EQUIPMENT: Yes

INSTRUCTION: Yes

FOOD FACILITIES: Cafeteria at the Ascutney Alpine area nearby

LODGING: Inns and motels in the area

HOW TO GET THERE: I–91 to Route 44 in Vermont; west to the touring center

This broad plateau looks down on the white-steepled village of Brownsville and beyond to the pretty white swaths of the Ascutney Alpine area, a tall tower of a peak. For tourers, the surroundings are lumpy and very pretty—the essence of Vermont's Green Mountain countryside. The 32 kilometers of trail undulate through this land over pastures, along stream beds, and through deep fir thickets. Nearly all of it is gentle until you take the guided backcountry tours—including overnight trips by arrangement—at which point the skiing becomes a bit of a challenge. At the warming hut and rental shop, skiers can arrange for lessons.

THE CATAMOUNT TRAIL ASSOCIATION
Box 897
Burlington, Vermont 05402

The core of the Catamount Trail Association (CTA) is a group of fanatic skiers who trekked the length of Vermont in March 1984 and who now dedicate themselves to the proposition that all skiers could and should ski on North America's longest trail—from Massachusetts to Quebec.

Steve Bushey, Paul Jarris, and Ben Rose hatched the idea that by linking the trails of several touring areas together with old roads along the ridge line of the Green Mountains, the entire length of the state can be easily traversed. The route selected is a skiing nirvana: a trail that runs through deep woods and open fields; over long descents down forgotten roads; over clearings with sudden views of mountain and valley; and down into amiable New England villages as you trek along north. The largest part of this "winter-long" trail, as its creators call it, is already accessible to skiers in the form of unplowed roads connected to groomed ski-center trails and other public ways. However, there are several sections that still must be cleared, and Catamount Trail Association members—present and future—are going about the task. Anyone who joins CTA (write at the above address) will be kept informed of developments by newsletter.

With an average elevation of between 1,500 and 2,000 feet, the trail system will have reliable snow cover and will constitute a skiing resource of every level of Nordic aficionado. The trail begins at the White House in Wilmington, Vermont, and roughly parallels Route 100 up to Hermitage, Stratton, Nordic Inn, and the Village Inn outside of Londonderry. The trek then pushes north over the Green Mountains toward Rutland, where it picks up Mountain Meadows near Killington; then Mountain Top, Blueberry Hill, Sugarbush, Tucker Hill, Camel's Hump, and the Trapp Family Lodge at Stowe along with Mansfield. From Mansfield, the tour pushes up on the 10th Army Mountain road to Top Notch, Edson Hill, Craftsbury, Hazen's Notch, and on to its terminus at Jay Peak.

SKI TOURS OF VERMONT

RFD 1
Chester, Vermont 05143
(802) 824–6012

HOW TO GET THERE: Massachusetts Turnpike to I–91 exit; follow to
Route 11 in Vermont

Rather than a particular destination, Ski Tours of Vermont is a guide
and instruction service in the National Forest of Weston and Londonderry, Vermont. Tours access the Great Vermont Ski Trail and
offer personalized outfitting and instruction. Treks vary from three
to eight days and put together inn-to-inn touring—the ultimate in
the trekking end of the sport—at its very best. Aside from encoun-
tering a variety of terrain types as you ski through the Green Mountains, you will stay at country inns—from old New England
farmhouses to former country gentlemen's estates—and sample all
sorts of cuisines, from French, to Swiss, to genuine New England.
Meanwhile your luggage is sent along to your next stop. Like most
ski-guide services, Ski Tours will match a trip to the skier's ability,
experience, and taste. But make plans early.

TATER HILL CROSS-COUNTRY SKI CENTER

Chester, Vermont 05143
(802) 875–2517

HOURS: 9:00 A.M. to 4:30 P.M.
TRAIL SYSTEM: 40 kilometers (about 25 miles)
TRAIL DIFFICULTY: Easiest, more difficult, most difficult
TRAIL GROOMING: Over about 20 kilometers
RENTAL EQUIPMENT: Yes
INSTRUCTION: Yes
FOOD FACILITIES: On the premises
LODGING: Within 3 miles
HOW TO GET THERE: Follow I–91 to Exit 6; Route 103 heading north
to Chester; then Route 11 going west to the center, between
Chester and Londonderry

Tater Hill Center is a good-sized trail system surrounding a 200-year-old farmhouse in central Vermont. It offers good skiing on groomed trails, as well as some real wilderness experience breaking trail as you ski out to the tough Williams River loop. To get your bearings first, the Whitetail and Sweet Potater trails are flat running loops, both of which pass warming shelters along the way. Most trails pass through hardwood forest with some nice views of the rolling Green Mountain foothills. Back at the inn, food and drink are available in the post-Revolutionary flavor of so many Vermont inns. Through the season there are several races organized, along with the annual Scandinavian Night, a moonlight cruise followed by an embarrassment of caloric riches at the smorgasbord table.

MOUNTAIN TOP CROSS-COUNTRY SKI CENTER

Chittenden, Vermont 05737
(802) 483–6089

HOURS: 9:00 A.M. to 5:00 P.M.

TRAIL SYSTEM: 110 kilometers (about 70 miles); all but 20 kilometers groomed for skating

TRAIL DIFFICULTY: Easiest, more difficult, most difficult

TRAIL GROOMING: When fully open, 70 kilometers groomed daily. One side double track, one side groomed for skating

RENTAL EQUIPMENT: 125 sets

INSTRUCTION: PSIA-certified

FOOD FACILITIES: Snack bar at the touring center; full-service restaurant at the Mountain Top Inn

LODGING: Mountain Top Inn, a full-service hotel with fifty rooms

HOW TO GET THERE: I–93 to I–89; take Exit 1 and Route 4 traveling west to Rutland. Follow signs for Mountain Top Cross-Country Ski Center just past the entrance to Pico Peak.

Just when you think you've seen all of Vermont's country inns and ski-touring areas, there is another inn, another area more beautiful than the last. That's the first impression one gets from Mountain Top, with its enormous trail system that winds out through dazzling

white meadows and quiet hardwood forest land. The elevation—2,000 feet—gives Mountain Top excellent capacity to hold snow as well as some stunning panoramic views of the peaks and lakes of the Green Mountain National Forest. In addition, Mountain Top makes its own snow on a 5-kilometer track loop that is a fine warm-up and exercise area for all ability levels. Beyond that, there is skiing over the gently rolling Alpine meadows and spruce forest and then some toe-curling challenge for experts over tough, twisting, choppy trails with steep verticals. The ski season holds well into the spring here.

At day's end, the Ski Shop, a converted horse barn warmed by a big wood stove, has a full complement of retail and rental gear, hot soups, drinks, and snacks. There is also a sun deck for the mild days. Skiers can sign up here for lessons, waxing and racing clinics, seminars, and films. Remember that the area is near two big down-hill centers (Pico and Killington), so visitors should seek advance reservations.

CRAFTSBURY NORDIC SKI CENTER

Box 31
Craftsbury Common, Vermont 05827
(802) 586–7767

HOURS: 9:00 A.M. to 5:00 P.M. (night skiing under the lights)

TRAIL SYSTEM: 65 kilometers (about 40 miles)

TRAIL DIFFICULTY: Easiest, more difficult, most difficult

TRAIL GROOMING: Daily. Single trackset and skating lanes

RENTAL EQUIPMENT: Yes

INSTRUCTION: Private and group lessons

FOOD FACILITIES: Buffet-style dining—three meals

LODGING: Ski dorm, apartments, cottages, and fifty other units at the center

HOW TO GET THERE: I–89 to Montpelier, Vermont; Route 14 to Craftsbury

Located in one of the wildest stretches of New England—the Northeast Kingdom—Craftsbury's 65 kilometers of trails, including a full skating track, are groomed to a fault and are maintained for racing as well as casual recreational skiing. The trail system winds into others in the region, accessing about 110 kilometers and encompassing the entire town of Craftsbury. Two other fine New England inns are located along the trail system.

With one of the longest seasons in the East—November to April—Craftsbury offers excellent skiing over the whole ability range, from beginners to serious veterans and racers. Children are welcome at all facilities at Craftsbury.

BURKE MOUNTAIN SKI TOURING CENTER

RR1, Box 62A
East Burke, Vermont 05832
(802) 626–8338

HOURS: 9:00 A.M. to sunset
TRAIL SYSTEM: 53 kilometers (about 31 miles)
TRAIL DIFFICULTY: Easiest, more difficult, most difficult
TRAIL GROOMING: Yes. One half groomed for skating
RENTAL EQUIPMENT: Yes
INSTRUCTION: PSIA-certified
FOOD FACILITIES: Snack bar at touring center
LODGING: At nearby inns and condominiums
HOW TO GET THERE: I–91 traveling north to Exit 23; Route 5 to Route 114 to East Burke; signs to Burke Mountain

This historic center for Alpine athletes (Burke Ski Academy) also maintains a well-developed touring center over the rolling meadows and deep Vermont woodlands near the Northeast Wilderness Kingdom. Most of the trail system is intermediate, though those same trails have been used for National Cross-Country Championships. From some high-country vantage points, skiers look out for miles to the west and can view the striking scenery of Willoughby Gap, gateway to the Northeast Kingdom. Skiers may use any trail system here and wind back to the center. The Touring Center itself is a friendly, bustling stop in an old restored farmhouse with a radiant wood stove at its center. Here skiers may sip hot cider and homemade soups, rent equipment, buy retail goods, and seek instruction. Children are welcome both at the touring center and at the Cutter Inn, in the midst of the trail network.

BLUEBERRY HILL CROSS-COUNTRY SKI CENTER

RD 3
Goshen, Vermont 05733
(802) 247–6735 or (800) 274–6535;
outside Vermont: (800) 448–0707

HOURS: 8:30 A.M. to dusk

TRAIL SYSTEM: 50 to 75 kilometers (about 30 to 47 miles), depending on snow cover and forestry activity in the National Forest

TRAIL DIFFICULTY: Easiest, more difficult, most difficult

TRAIL GROOMING: All trails groomed and double trackset. Some skating lanes

RENTAL EQUIPMENT: Yes

INSTRUCTION: Private and group rates

FOOD FACILITIES: Soup included in the trail fee, along with "munchies," but bring your own packed lunches and other meals

LODGING: Blueberry Hill is connected with a small inn

HOW TO GET THERE: I–91 to I–89 heading west to Route 4, west to Rutland, Vermont; north on Route 7 to Brandon, east on Route 73 to Goshen, then left at the town hall to Blueberry Hill

Blueberry Hill, nestled in the Green Mountain National Forest with an honest 50- to 75-kilometer trail system, is a major ski area for the serious tourer as well as the hiker searching for gorgeous mountain overlooks that plunge into deep forest land with snow-laden fir boughs and frozen brooks. Silver Lake trail is a good way to get your legs; then stretch out along Long Trail for more challenging skiing. There is an excellent retail and rental shop at Blueberry, along with waxing rooms where some helpful lessons are given. The inn is small—just eight rooms—but the space is worth fighting for.

Ask for owner Tony Clark for special advice about skiing conditions.

GRAFTON PONDS CROSS-COUNTRY SKI CENTER

The Old Tavern at Grafton
Grafton, Vermont 05146
(802) 843–2231

HOURS: 9:00 A.M. to 4:00 P.M.

TRAIL SYSTEM: About 30 kilometers (18 miles)

TRAIL DIFFICULTY: Easiest, more difficult, most difficult

TRAIL GROOMING: All trails groomed and trackset, with skating lanes provided

RENTAL EQUIPMENT: Full rental facility

INSTRUCTION: Private lessons by appointment

FOOD FACILITIES: Formal dining at The Old Tavern with trail snacks available at the center

LODGING: The Old Tavern has several guest rooms; there are also several motels in the area

HOW TO GET THERE: From I–91 take Exit 5 and head west on Route 121. Grafton Ponds is located at the intersection of Routes 121 and 35

This area is one of several in Vermont that combines a rich outback experience with modern grooming techniques on the trail and a rustic country inn with gourmet dining after the skiing ends. The trail system has something for everyone, starting with the beginners' and warm-up loops like Strider and Windham Pond Trail: level skiing on broad swaths for confidence-building and loosening. For the intermediate there is the 3-mile New Lee Wilson Trail that meanders through forested hillsides and the 2-mile Warren Chivers Trail that combines a short uphill with a gentler, undulating downhill. The Dinkum-Dankum Area has lots of moderate terrain with the infamous Gorge thrown in to give a sobering snap of reality to anyone nodding off or feeling smug. This latter area has all sorts of surprises and payoffs—like Mathey Lane, an extremely pleasing .7-mile run that brings skiers home after taking the dreaded plunge.

The Old Tavern is a graceful old stagecoach inn dating back to 1801. Restored antique guest rooms and elegant inn dining make this one of Vermont's best bets for destination skiers.

HIGHLAND LODGE

RR1, Box 1290
Greensboro, Vermont 05841
(802) 533–2647

HOURS: 9:00 A.M. to 5:00 P.M.

TRAIL SYSTEM: About 70 kilometers (42 miles)

TRAIL DIFFICULTY: Easiest, more difficult

TRAIL GROOMING: All 42 miles are roller-packed, 5 feet in width; 10 miles are double trackset

RENTAL EQUIPMENT: Yes

INSTRUCTION: PSIA-certified

FOOD FACILITIES: Full meals plus trail snacks in the ski shop

LODGING: Eleven rooms at the lodge and two cottages

HOW TO GET THERE: I–91 to St. Johnsbury; at Exit 15, Route 2 heading west 10 miles to West Danville; northwest on Route 15 to Route 16; north on Route 16 to East Hardwick, then west to Greensboro

There are three loops to Highland Lodge's trail system, two are 5 miles and another is 15 miles. All of these course through the gently rolling pasturelands and evergreen woods that lead down and sweep the shore of Caspian Lake. The system covers about 25 square miles. Both loops offer some wonderful overlooks of this lake region and end with a downhill stretch toward a drink at the fireplace. The trails are conscientiously roller-packed so skiers don't have to bushwhack their way through deep powder or crust.

The lodge is a spectacular stately Vermont inn with a broad homey dining room, library and lounge areas, and good-size double bedrooms. There is room for thirty-five guests. The inn hosts loyal families that have been returning for several years. There is also a thorough ski and rental shop at the center where skiers may sign up for instruction and guided tours of the region.

CAMEL'S HUMP NORDIC SKI CENTER

Box 422, RFD 1
Huntington, Vermont 05462
(802) 434–2704

HOURS: 9:00 A.M. to 5:00 P.M.

TRAIL SYSTEM: 65 kilometers (about 40 miles)

TRAIL DIFFICULTY: Easiest, more difficult, most difficult

TRAIL GROOMING: As needed; 30 kilometers of skating lanes

RENTAL EQUIPMENT: Yes

INSTRUCTION: Yes

FOOD FACILITIES: Snacks served at the center

LODGING: Bed-and-breakfast on premises; other lodging nearby

HOW TO GET THERE: I–91 to I–89 northwest to Exit 11; 7 miles south to Huntington; 3 miles east from Huntington village to the touring center

Of all Vermont's high Alpine ski touring, this Nordic Ski Center just may provide the most dramatic and unusual experience. Though the center itself is a modest, family-run operation, it is located at road's end high in the eastern foothills of the 4,000-foot Camel's Hump and accesses many miles of wilderness as well as providing its own well-groomed trail system of about 37 miles. Here is skiing for everyone: the high-energy seeker of wilderness adventure can find guided overnight trips to a snow cave. One trail, the Honey Hollow Ski Trail, climbs to 1,900 feet, then drops 1,500 feet over the west slope on a nonstop downhill run of 9 kilometers to the bank of the Winooski River in Bolton. Skiers needn't climb back up this 5-mile rush through the state forest; the center provides shuttle service back home again. The center intends to complete soon a network of trail huts for overnight skiers who can travel south to Breadloaf and Blueberry Hill.

For gentler spirits not looking for quite this level of stimulation, the center has plenty of cruising on flatter trails through woods and open mountain uplands. All rentals and retail needs, along with meals, are taken care of in the rustic center, which now also provides lodging.

JAY PEAK SKI AREA
Route 242
Jay, Vermont 05859
(802) 988–2611 (Customer Service)

HOURS: 8:30 A.M. to dusk

TRAIL SYSTEM: About 20 kilometers (13 miles)

TRAIL DIFFICULTY: Easiest, more difficult, most difficult

TRAIL GROOMING: As needed

RENTAL EQUIPMENT: 50 sets

INSTRUCTION: PSIA-certified

FOOD FACILITIES: Cafeteria and two restaurants

LODGING: Hotel Jay. Call Jay Peak Lodging Association at (800) 451–4449, or (802) 988–2611

HOW TO GET THERE: I–91 to Exit 26 in Orleans, Vermont; northwest via Routes 5 to 14 to 100, to 101, and to 242 and the entrance

With its multinational flag row, its mix of languages and cultures, and its large Alpine facility, Jay Peak, in the northern most tip of the state in the Wilderness Kingdom, is a most exciting place to spend a ski weekend or vacation. The extensive cross-country trail system incorporates the lower half of Jay Mountain itself, which brings into play some long, gradually pitched Alpine runouts from mid-mountain down to the base. Obviously, Jay is a fine place to work on Telemark skiing, for then skiers can make use of the entire area— including two T-bars (included in trail fee) when none of your cross-country purist pals are watching. The base lodge and restaurant at the Hotel Jay is ample and well stocked. As a diversion from skiing, take the aerial tram to the top of one of the most overwhelming mountain vistas anywhere, as you view the sun dropping toward the Laurentians and Montreal. Don't worry—if you're not up to skiing down the mountain on skinny skis, you may take the tram back down.

STERLING RIDGE INN

RR1, Box 578C
Jeffersonville, Vermont 05464
(802) 644–8265

HOURS: 8:00 A.M. to 5:00 P.M.

TRAIL SYSTEM: 20 kilometers (about 12 miles)

TRAIL DIFFICULTY: Easiest, more difficult, most difficult

TRAIL GROOMING: Groomed and trackset

RENTAL EQUIPMENT: No

INSTRUCTION: No

FOOD FACILITIES: Breakfast and lunch (or trail-packed lunch) daily from the inn; gourmet dinner prepared Monday, Wednesday, and Saturday evenings through ski season

LODGING: Eight rooms at the inn; shared or private baths available

HOW TO GET THERE: Route I–89 to Burlington, then Route 15 to Jeffersonville. From Jeffersonville, 1.2 miles east on Route 15, then
right on the dirt road for 1.1 miles; then south on Route 108;
turn left by the Red Fox onto an unpaved road for 2.1 miles

The Sterling Ridge Inn is one of the many fine four-season Vermont
inns that maintain a well-groomed cross-country trail system for winter guests. It is located near the renowned cross-country and alpine
skiing activity of the Stowe area, so skiers staying at Sterling Ridge
have many other skiing options in addition to the inn's own 12-kilo-
meter trail system. The skiing at the inn ranges from flattish open-
meadow trails that let novices get their bearings to a few more
challenging trail loops, one of which leads out to a cabin in the
woods along an intermediate trail. Skiers out for the day can take
packed lunches from the gourmet kitchen at the inn and return after
the most vigorous day of skiing without fear of a calorie deficit. Three
nights a week the inn offers its own dinner; otherwise there are several restaurants in the area. Downhill skiing is also available nearby.

MOUNTAIN MEADOWS CROSS-COUNTRY SKI CENTER

Box 2080
Killington, Vermont 05751
(802) 775-7077

HOURS: 8:00 A.M. to 6:00 P.M.

TRAIL SYSTEM: 40 kilometers (25 miles)

TRAIL DIFFICULTY: Easiest, more difficult, most difficult

TRAIL GROOMING: Daily grooming on all 40 kilometers; 15 kilometers of skating lanes

RENTAL EQUIPMENT: Yes

INSTRUCTION: PSIA-certified

FOOD FACILITIES: Lunches and snacks at the center

LODGING: Dormitory and private rooms at the center

HOW TO GET THERE: I–93 to I–89 to Exit 2, then west on Route 4 to Killington; right on Thundering Brook Road to Mountain Meadows

Nestled in a high mountain valley 5 miles away from the famous Killington downhill area, the Mountain Meadows Lodge is a large century-old converted farmhouse and barn that now can accommodate seventy tourers. The trail network, combining the depths of the Green Mountain National Forest with open mountain highlands and the flats of Kent's Pond, has offerings for every ability level. The adventurous can pick up the route along the 40-mile Catamount Ski Touring Trail and follow it into Chittenden to the Mountain Top Ski Touring Center. The shop at Mountain Meadows is fully equipped with rentals and retail gear, a waxing room, and good advice. Skiers can sign up here for day or moonlight tours. Beginners should ask about the Five-Day Learn-to-Ski Week. Two kilometers near the lodge are lighted for some night running.

NORDIC INN SKI TOURING CENTER
Route 11
Landgrove, Vermont 05148
(802) 824–6444

HOURS: 9:00 A.M. to 4:00 P.M.
TRAIL SYSTEM: About 26 kilometers (15-plus miles)
TRAIL DIFFICULTY: Easiest, more difficult, most difficult
TRAIL GROOMING: Trackset daily
RENTAL EQUIPMENT: 50 sets
INSTRUCTION: Yes
FOOD FACILITIES: Gourmet restaurant (seats 75) and pub at the inn
LODGING: Four rooms at the inn; other motels nearby
HOW TO GET THERE: I–91 to Exit 6; Route 103 traveling northwest; then Route 11 heading west to Landgrove and the inn

With its continental French cuisine and pub life, Nordic Inn is becoming as well known for its après-ski life as for its excellent trail system. The latter, a thoroughly groomed and trackset web of trails at more than 1,369 feet, leads skiers into the Green National Forest, where plenty of wilderness skiing is at hand. The inn offers a full service of guided tours, instruction, and various events through the season. After a day on these broad, hardwood-lined trails, skiers stretch in front of the huge fieldstone fireplace that crackles and roars through the long winter evenings. This is a fine destination area for those who like some pampering when they're off the trails. Nordic Inn is just 3 miles from Londonderry and 5 miles from the Bromley downhill ski area.

VIKING SKI TOURING CENTRE

Little Pond Road, RR Box 70
Londonderry, Vermont 05148
(802) 824–3933

HOURS: 8:30 A.M. to 4:30 P.M.

TRAIL SYSTEM: 30 kilometers (18 miles)

TRAIL DIFFICULTY: Easiest, more difficult, most difficult

TRAIL GROOMING: Yes, trackset

RENTAL EQUIPMENT: 80 sets

INSTRUCTION: PSIA-certified

FOOD FACILITIES: Meals at the cafe; hot snacks and drinks at the ski center

LODGING: Inns and hotels in the area

HOW TO GET THERE: I–91 to Brattleboro, Vermont; Route 30 going northwest, then north on Route 100 to Londonderry

Viking is one of the original New England touring centers, dating back to 1970. It has a variety of offerings for skiers of all levels and, like most well-established centers, really emphasizes the proper education of a skier. The trail system is absolutely superb, with intelligently cut and marked trails for every level, and with guided tours out to beautiful remote backlands near Grout Pond in the Green Mountains' Lye Brook Wilderness Area.

Just as it should, the center fixes on skier needs: A complete rental and retail facility is available, along with a waxing room and a warming shack and plenty of advice and discussion about the potion of the day. Lodging and expanded dining facilities are available at any number of inns and hotels in the Manchester/Londonderry area.

RABBIT HILL INN

Lower Waterford, Vermont 05848
(802) 748–5168

HOURS: Dawn to dusk

TRAIL SYSTEM: 25 kilometers (about 16 miles)

TRAIL DIFFICULTY: Easiest, more difficult

TRAIL GROOMING: Yes

RENTAL EQUIPMENT: Yes

INSTRUCTION: Limited (call ahead)

FOOD FACILITIES: Breakfast and dinner

LODGING: Twenty rooms with private baths; some with working fireplaces

HOW TO GET THERE: Route 18 from Littleton, New Hampshire, to St. Johnsbury, Vermont; then 6 miles from the termination of I–93

Rabbit Hill's trails meander along the Connecticut River, through groves of beechwoods, past beaver lodges, and up Rabbit Hill for a look back over the picturesque village anchored by a white New England meeting house. This is quiet, high-quality skiing away from the masses. Trails cross much private land, looping through wide meadows that plunge into forested river banks. The 1795 inn with its twenty bedrooms once served one hundred horse teams daily that hauled produce from Portland, Maine, to interior New England and Montreal. Nearly all the rooms have mountain views, and the cuisine, enhanced by offerings from the inn's own wine cellar, is exquisite. Aside from skiing, the inn provides guided nature walks and climbs in the White Mountains.

FOX RUN CROSS-COUNTRY SKI CENTER
RFD 1, Box 123
Ludlow, Vermont 05149
(802) 228–8871

HOURS: 8:00 A.M. to 5:00 P.M.

TRAIL SYSTEM: 20 kilometers (about 12 miles)

TRAIL DIFFICULTY: Easiest, more difficult, most difficult

TRAIL GROOMING: Yes. Some lanes for skating

RENTAL EQUIPMENT: Yes

INSTRUCTION: Yes

FOOD FACILITIES: Lunch and dinner

LODGING: At the Winchester Inn, owned by Fox Run, and the Okemo Inn across the street; other areas have bed-and-breakfast lodging

HOW TO GET THERE: Route I–91 to Exit 6, then north on Route 103 to Ludlow. One mile north of Okemo access road

The Fox Run Cross-Country Ski Center has grown in trail size over the years, so that it now qualifies as a moderately large area with a full-range system through fir-forested terrain that gives skiers some nice views of Okemo Mountain. The trails vary from flat racers to choppy bushwhacking and serious verticals for the expert skier. There is also now a full rental and retail shop on the premises, as well as instructors who will help you bone up on racing technique or take you on a guided tour of the network. In the inn, the wood beams glowing with the light from copper lamps make a nice ambiance in which to loosen down from the day's skiing.

HILDENE SKI TOURING CENTER

Box 377
Manchester, Vermont 05254
(802) 362–1788

HOURS: 9:00 A.M. to 4:00 P.M.

TRAIL SYSTEM: 21 kilometers (about 13 miles)

TRAIL DIFFICULTY: Easiest, more difficult, most difficult

TRAIL GROOMING: All groomed, 10 kilometers trackset; some skating lanes

RENTAL EQUIPMENT: Yes

INSTRUCTION: Private and group by arrangement

FOOD FACILITIES: Hot soups and cocoa all week

LODGING: Motels and inns nearby

HOW TO GET THERE: Route 30 traveling north to Manchester Center, Vermont; left onto Route 7A heading south. Touring center is ½ mile on left, beyond Equinox Hotel.

This historic estate was built by Robert Todd Lincoln, son of President Abraham Lincoln. It is a 412-acre estate with trails meandering about a central warming hut in the old Carriage Barn. One trail features long downhill runs on a gradual slope, and the fields are open for skating. There is something here for the veteran skier as well as the novice, and all phases in between. Special events beyond the skiing include tours of the main house at Christmastime, December 27 to 29.

CARROL AND JANE RIKERT SKI TOURING CENTER

Service Building
Middlebury College
Middlebury, Vermont 05073

HOURS: 9:00 A.M. to 4:00 P.M.

TRAIL SYSTEM: 50 kilometers (about 30 miles)

TRAIL DIFFICULTY: Easiest, more difficult, most difficult

TRAIL GROOMING: Groomed and trackset. Skating lanes

RENTAL EQUIPMENT: Yes

INSTRUCTION: Yes

FOOD FACILITIES: Light snacks and hot drinks at the center; restaurants within 5 miles

LODGING: Hotels and motels in the area, within 13 miles of the touring center

HOW TO GET THERE: I–93 to I–89 to Route 100 in Bethel, Vermont; east on Route 125 east in Hancock

The annual Middlebury Winter Carnival Nordic events are staged at this highly manicured touring center—an indication of the quality of the trail system and the grooming, marking, and care of the trails. Set in the Breadloaf Campus at Middlebury, the trails course around the Robert Frost Memorial here in the base of the Green Mountains. Some trails run out to the Snow Bowl, and one direction links up with the Blueberry Hill Cross-Country Ski Center trail system. This area is largely for intermediate skiing with some gentle flats available, too. There are waxes available along with rental and retail gear at the center. A warming hut is on the premises; they serve superb soups.

ALPINE HAVEN

Montgomery Center, Vermont 05471
(802) 326–4567

HOURS: 9:00 A.M. to 4:00 P.M.

TRAIL SYSTEM: 24 kilometers (15 miles)

TRAIL DIFFICULTY: Easiest, more difficult, most difficult

TRAIL GROOMING: Groomed by snowmobile

RENTAL EQUIPMENT: No, but nearby

INSTRUCTION: No, but nearby

FOOD FACILITIES: Restaurant nearby

LODGING: At the Alpine Meadows Hotel, the Hotel Jay, or among the several chalets in the area

HOW TO GET THERE: I–91 to Orleans, Vermont, exit; then Route 105 to Route 101 to the Alpine Haven Condos between Jay Center and Montgomery Center

To the southwest of Jay Peak, bordering on the immense Northeast Wilderness Kingdom, Alpine Haven offers a landscape of cruising over gentle rollers to the more hilly ruggedness along the side of Jay Peak's alpine terrain. This is secluded skiing in the true northern wilderness, though Telemarkers who wish to practice have the aerial tram at Jay Peak and some long, smooth runouts down the green-circle Alpine trails.

Nearby, the Hotel Jay has fine accommodations for the destination skier, too. This is a region peopled with many Montrealers, and the whole area has a pleasant international feel.

HAZEN'S NOTCH CROSS-COUNTRY SKI CENTER
Route 58
Montgomery Center, Vermont 05471
(802) 326–4708

HOURS: 9:00 A.M. to 4:30 P.M.

TRAIL SYSTEM: 50 kilometers (about 30 miles) of groomed trails with 75 kilometers of backcountry trails

TRAIL DIFFICULTY: Easiest, more difficult, most difficult

TRAIL GROOMING: Groomed and trackset as needed. Limited skating

RENTAL EQUIPMENT: Yes

INSTRUCTION: Much individual attention for novice skiers; special introductory clinics for Telemark skiing

FOOD FACILITIES: At the ski chalet

LODGING: Overnight accommodations at the guest house at the ski center; inns and motels within 1½ miles

HOW TO GET THERE: Route I–91 to White River Junction, Vermont; I–89 to Waterbury, Vermont; north on Route 100 to Eden, then Route 118 to Montgomery Center; east on Route 58 to Hazen's

Nestled high in the wild country and heavy snow belt of the Northeast Kingdom, nearly 75 kilometers of trails wind through a mosaic of deep fir forest and mountain meadowland. These fields provide spectacular views of several mountain ranges, while the backcountry trails lead to little villages and into the dramatic Hazen's Notch. Skiers can find lodging at the center where a guest house offers warm, friendly surroundings that seem a haven after skiing in these winter wilds. After a drink and hot homemade food, high-energy skiers can go back out on guided moonlight tours. Lamps are provided. Telemark clinics and slopes for practice are also available. The Touring Center has a wonderful French/English mix that gives this Green Mountain jewel the kind of international feeling that Alpine skiers find at Jay Peak.

VERMONT VOYAGER EXPEDITIONS

Route 242, Box 1010
Montgomery Center, Vermont 05471
(802) 326–4789

"VVE," as its students call it, is not a touring area as such but rather a year-round mountaineering school associated with Jay Peak in the Northeast Wilderness Kingdom in the northern part of the state. It also is part of an elaborate inn-to-inn touring system that is part of the Northern Frontier Ski Region of Vermont.

VVE, founded in 1980, is dedicated to "the conservation of wilderness through the education of its users." VVE provides instruction in the practical end of wilderness skiing, giving individuals or groups the confidence to explore this exciting corner of the sport of cross-country skiing. Before skiers can try the wilderness experience, they must learn it, which means it must be taught. That is what VVE is all about. Skiers can use VVE for their destination,

then, under the tutelege of expert outdoorsmen and guides, undertake as much or as little as they feel up to in this vast unspoiled terrain among the northernmost peaks of the Green Mountains, as well as the lowland trails that lead through meadows and farms and in and out of remote northern villages.

AMISKI SKI AREA

RR # 1, Box 600
Moretown, Vermont 05673
(802) 244–5677

HOURS: Daily
TRAIL SYSTEM: 15 kilometers (about 9 miles); backcountry skiing
TRAIL DIFFICULTY: Easiest, more difficult, most difficult
TRAIL GROOMING: 15 kilometer groomed and tracked; 1 kilometer lighted for night skiing
RENTAL EQUIPMENT: Yes
INSTRUCTION: Yes, PSIA lessons
FOOD FACILITIES: Full meals and snacks at the barn
LODGING: Room for eighteen skiers in the barn; motels and inns nearby
HOW TO GET THERE: Follow Route 93 heading north to Route 89 traveling west. Take exit 9 then follow Route 100 going south for 10 miles. Look for signs when you get to Moretown.

This unique ski area centers around a beautifully restored Vermont barn where skiers live and dine between forays out around the hilly countryside of the central Green Mountains. The trail system begins on a farm meadow, then winds through hardwood and evergreen forests. While many of the trail choices are suitable for inexperienced skiers, Amiski also has some challenging and hilly skiing for advanced practitioners of the sport, including guided backcountry tours in the Green Mountain terrain. This feature of the area draws both the experienced skier and the intermediate skier looking for extraordinary adventure beyond the confines of a groomed set of tracks. This is an area that fills the needs of most skiers and places a heavy emphasis on the family ski experience.

PROSPECT MOUNTAIN SKI TOURING CENTER

HCR 65 - Box 760
Old Bennington, Vermont 05201
(802) 442–2575

HOURS: 9:00 A.M. to 5:00 P.M.

TRAIL SYSTEM: 40 kilometers (18 miles)

TRAIL DIFFICULTY: Easiest, more difficult, most difficult

TRAIL GROOMING: All tracks are groomed and skateable

RENTAL EQUIPMENT: 85 sets

INSTRUCTION: Yes

FOOD FACILITIES: Lunch only served at the base lodge

LODGING: Greenwood Lodge nearby accommodates groups; motels in the area

HOW TO GET THERE: Eight miles east of Bennington; 12 miles west of Wilmington on Route 9

A high-altitude ski touring center (2,150 feet) in the Green Mountains of western Vermont, Prospect Mountain usually retains a snow cover after the flatlands are bare. The area offers as wide a variety as any ski area in New England—from flat running tracks, to wilderness bushwhacking on 20 kilometers of expert terrain on the mountainside. Another 10 kilometers are intermediate; and 10 kilometers are easiest.

Groomed tracks break down to roughly 5 kilometers of most difficult and 10 of more difficult.

WILD WINGS CROSS-COUNTRY SKI CENTER

Peru, Vermont 05152
(802) 824–6793

HOURS: 9:00 A.M. to 4:00 P.M.

TRAIL SYSTEM: 25 kilometers (about 16 miles)

TRAIL DIFFICULTY: Easiest, more difficult, most difficult

TRAIL GROOMING: Groomed and trackset as needed

RENTAL EQUIPMENT: Yes

INSTRUCTION: PSIA-certified

FOOD FACILITIES: Hot drinks and snacks in the warming rooms and at nearby restaurants

LODGING: Tourers can find inns and motels within 3 to 10 miles

HOW TO GET THERE: I–91 to Brattleboro, Vermont; Route 30 northwest to Route 11, east to Peru; left at the Peru Church and follow to Wild Wings

Still in the Green Mountain National Forest, this is a small, extremely cozy sort of area out of some of the touring bustle or the hotshot race crowd in skin-tight suits. In a converted horse barn you'll find a rental shop and warming/waxing room, then go out skiing over 10 to 12 miles of groomed trails. This system feeds into the vast Green Mountain trail system as well. This home of the wild turkey is one of the prettiest ski regions in New England.

WILDERNESS TRAILS AND NORDIC SKI SCHOOL

c/o The Quechee Inn
Quechee, Vermont 05059
(802) 295–7620; Off-season, (802) 295–3133.

HOURS: 9:00 A.M. to dark

TRAIL SYSTEM: 15 kilometers (about 9 miles)

TRAIL DIFFICULTY: Easiest, more difficult, most difficult

TRAIL GROOMING: Machine trackset

RENTAL EQUIPMENT: Yes

INSTRUCTION: Two PSIA-certified instructors

FOOD FACILITIES: A trailside restaurant, Red Pines, serves hot chocolate, coffee, and snacks. Breakfast and dinner are available at the inn

LODGING: Twenty-two units at the inn; other motels nearby

HOW TO GET THERE: I–93 north to I–89; at White River Junction, Exit 1; Route 4 west toward Woodstock, and follow signs to Quechee. At the sign, turn right onto Clubhouse Road; travel 1 mile to the inn.

The touring at Quechee is among the most beautiful anywhere, with the most spectacular trail running along the rim of Quechee Gorge. Here, a waterfall plunges 165 feet down into the gorge. Skiers are treated to a wildlife area where sightings of mink, otter, beaver, fox, and porcupines are common. For birders, there are rare pileated woodpeckers in the trees, as well as owls that are sometimes encountered on moonlight tours. Ask for Marty Banak for tips on the wildlife tour. Generally, Wilderness Trails is a nice low-key sort of area known mostly for its emphasis on teaching. In the Woodstock area, there is plenty of skiing (both Nordic and Alpine); the whole region offers nightlife and shopping.

GREEN MOUNTAIN CROSS-COUNTRY SKI AREA

At the Three Stallion Inn
Randolph, Vermont 05060
(802) 728–5575

HOURS: Dawn to dusk

TRAIL SYSTEM: 35 kilometers (about 21 miles)

TRAIL DIFFICULTY: Easiest, more difficult, most difficult

TRAIL GROOMING: Daily. Trackset and skating track

RENTAL EQUIPMENT: Yes

INSTRUCTION: Yes

FOOD FACILITIES: Meals served to guests in the farmhouse

LODGING: Fifteen rooms at the farmhouse, other inns and motels in the area

HOW TO GET THERE: I–93 to I–89 traveling north to Exit 4; then west on Route 66; left on Stock Farm Road to the touring center

The Green Mountain Touring Center is one of those no-nonsense, homey resorts that call to skiers who seek the simplicity of a fine trail system, good hot homemade food, and plenty of hospitality in a Victorian farmhouse inn. This center seems to weed out the essential pleasures of the sport from the frills that merely cost money and get in the way. Skiers at Green Mountain will find a big, conscientiously groomed and marked trail system spread out on nearly

1,400 acres of Green Mountain forest land where more than a few U.S. Ski Team members have trained over the years. The terrain rolls along gentle ridges and plunges into woods that can offer skiers any level of vertical ups and downs. For novices there are plenty of flat trails as well. At the center are a cocktail lounge and restaurant open to the public at lunch and dinner. Look into this inn as a four-season destination.

NORDIC ADVENTURES

Connie and Dean Mendell
Box 155, RFD 1
Rochester, Vermont 05767
(802) 767–3996

HOURS: To be arranged

TRAIL SYSTEM: Any and all accessible lands can be used

TRAIL DIFFICULTY: Easiest, more difficult

TRAIL GROOMING: Foot-packed or groomed with snowmobile

RENTAL EQUIPMENT: 50 sets of waxable backcountry skis

INSTRUCTION: PSIA-certified instructor

FOOD FACILITIES: A country lunch is offered on guided tours

LODGING: Inns in the area

HOW TO GET THERE: I–93 to I–89 north to the exit at Bethel, Vermont; then Route 107 to Route 100 north. The Mendell's house is 4 miles south of Rochester Village on Route 100 North

Nordic Adventures is an outfitter and guide system that offers personalized instruction on a one-to-one basis. Skiers interested in backcountry forays have a choice of several package plans, including inn-to-inn ski hikes, Norpine instruction, and moonlight escapades. A typical five-day package would include lodging, all meals, guide and instruction fees, luggage transfer, taxes, and gratuities. This is a different approach to touring than the ordinary destination trip and should appeal to skiers who really like to probe into the woolly corners of the sport. Mr. Mendell knows the woods and can personally arrange a wilderness tour to fit individual skiers' tastes and abilities.

TRAIL HEAD CROSS-COUNTRY SKI AREA

Star Route
Stockbridge, Vermont 05772
(802) 746–8038

HOURS: 9:00 A.M. to 5:00 P.M.

TRAIL SYSTEM: 45 kilometers (about 28 miles)

TRAIL DIFFICULTY: Easiest, more difficult, most difficult

TRAIL GROOMING: Partially; machine-set on beginner to intermediate terrain; most of the expert trails foot-packed

RENTAL EQUIPMENT: Yes

INSTRUCTION: Yes

FOOD FACILITIES: Homemade soups, snacks, drinks, and sandwiches in the lodge. Restaurants in the area for dinners

LODGING: Seven lodging establishments within five minutes of the area

HOW TO GET THERE: I–93 to I–89 to Route 107 in Vermont; then south onto Route 100 for 1 mile to the touring center

Near Rutland, Vermont, the Trail Head Touring Center is a large system in the Green Mountain National Forest offering a variety of touring experiences. Skiers can warm up with open-meadow cruising over well-set tracks, then roll down along the lovely Tweed River trails that course in and out of deep woods. More advanced skiers have the option of some real pumping terrain along the South Hill or out to the Liberty Hill System. Most of the ski terrain offers some nice glimpses of the nearby Alpine terrain. Back at the lodge, in a converted barn from the 1870s, cold, tired skiers lounge in front of the roaring fire sipping drinks and homemade soups. Here they find a complete rental and retail facility and can sign up for lessons with PSIA-certified instructors or citizen races. Also available are moonlit excursions through the river valley and over the pastureland. With Killington Ski Area nearby, there is plenty of nightlife for the indefatigable skier, as well as good lodging and dining. Trail Head is an excellent day or destination trip for skiers of every level.

EDSON HILL MANOR
Edson Hill Road
Stowe, Vermont 05672
(802) 253–7371

HOURS: 9:00 A.M. to 5:00 P.M.

TRAIL SYSTEM: 40 kilometers (25 miles)

TRAIL DIFFICULTY: Easiest, more difficult, most difficult

TRAIL GROOMING: Daily, as needed. Skating on 10 percent

RENTAL EQUIPMENT: Yes

INSTRUCTION: Yes

FOOD FACILITIES: At the Manor house

LODGING: Rooms of two to three beds at the Manor house

HOW TO GET THERE: I–91 and I–89 heading northwest to Exit 10; north on Route 100 to Stowe Village; Route 108 traveling west; take a right at the fork on Edson Hill Road to the Manor

This rather overlooked, under-publicized area has a mammoth trail system, few crowded days, and gorgeous terrain for first-out novices and old hands alike. The trails, spread out over a 400-acre estate, are contained in flat, gladed meadowland. Then the fun begins, as skiers climb off the flats, if they wish, into some backland touring in the rugged Green Mountain terrain. The wax shop is complete and has a nice feel of the horse barn that it serves as in the warm season. Here skiers can obtain retail gear of all kinds, rent skis, try to get words of free advice from the experts all around, or put down a little cash for a real lesson. The Edson Hill Manor itself is not quite in the character of the old Vermont inn tour, yet is extremely relaxing, gentle, and stress-removing. The food is fine, the atmosphere bright and supple. Also available to skiers is a country inn. Sleigh rides and horseback riding are available year-round.

MT. MANSFIELD SKI TOURING CENTER

Mountain Road
Stowe, Vermont 05672
(802) 253–7311, ext. 2243

HOURS: 9:00 A.M. to 4:00 P.M.

TRAIL SYSTEM: 50 kilometers (about 31 miles)

TRAIL DIFFICULTY: Easiest, more difficult, most difficult

TRAIL GROOMING: Grooming on 30 kilometers; unlimited wilderness access; skating

RENTAL EQUIPMENT: Yes

INSTRUCTION: Yes

FOOD FACILITIES: Full-service restaurant at the base lodge, and several restaurants on the road between Mansfield and Stowe. Snacks at the touring center

LODGING: At the Inn at the Mountain

HOW TO GET THERE: Route I–89 to Exit 10; then 10 miles north on Route 100 to Stowe Village; left on Route 108 for 5 miles

Always noted as one of the ski capitals of the East, Stowe's 50 kilometers of mapped Nordic trails (30 kilometers are groomed and trackset) live up to that reputation. Mt. Mansfield offers a variety of terrain for every ability level in acreage that plunges deep into the solitude and beauty of the Green Mountains. Because it intersects with other trail systems, skiers from Mt. Mansfield actually have 150 kilometers of trails at their disposal.

Using both sides of the historic Ranch Valley up the flanks of Mt. Mansfield, these trails are exceptionally well maintained, forming a complex that provides the basis for the famous Stowe Derby—an annual 12-mile trot from the top of Mansfield into the village of Stowe. Wilderness trails connect with the Trapp Family Lodge complex, allowing a full day of touring or wilderness exploration.

TOPNOTCH TOURING CENTER

Mountain Road
Stowe, Vermont 05672
(802) 253–8585

HOURS: 9:00 A.M. to 5:00 P.M.
TRAIL SYSTEM: 30 kilometers (about 20 miles)
TRAIL DIFFICULTY: Easiest, more difficult, most difficult
TRAIL GROOMING: 20 kilometers groomed daily; skating
RENTAL EQUIPMENT: Yes
INSTRUCTION: Yes
FOOD FACILITIES: The entire Stowe area is a culinary delight
LODGING: Dozens of inns and motels in the town of Stowe
HOW TO GET THERE: I–89 to Route 100 north; then northwest on
   Route 108. Topnotch is between Stowe Village and Mountain
   Mansfield, 4 miles from the village.

Like all ski centers of this region, the town of Stowe itself is the
draw here for the destination skier. Our advice is to book trips well
ahead, especially in busy seasons. The inn itself features lodging toward the luxury end of the spectrum and dining to match in this
very competitive restaurant area. The trail system, though it does
offer some trails in the "most difficult" category, is geared toward
less stressful skiing. The Lower and Upper Valley Trails send skiers
over some rugged terrain that eventually makes a link with Trapp
Lodge's trail system. Another route along some much easier terrain
ties skiers in with the Edson Hill Manor trails. Yet another route
(Cross Cut) winds skiers into the Mt. Mansfield downhill area for
some Telemark practice. For the less adventurous, the trails close to
the Topnotch Center itself are nicely groomed, gentle rollers that
run along open meadows, through woodland, and along the West
Branch River. Topnotch is an excellent spot for both the casual and
the more serious skier. For beginners there is an abundance of
open-field, flat skiing.

TRAPP FAMILY LODGE

Stowe, Vermont 05672
(802) 253–8511

HOURS: 9:00 A.M. to 5:00 P.M.

TRAIL SYSTEM: About 96 kilometers (60 miles)

TRAIL DIFFICULTY: Easiest, more difficult, most difficult

TRAIL GROOMING: Groomed and trackset on 60 kilometers; skating lanes

RENTAL EQUIPMENT: 400 sets

INSTRUCTION: PSIA-certied

FOOD FACILITIES: Restaurant and lounge; lunches served at cabin or on the trail system

LODGING: Ninety-three rooms on premises

HOW TO GET THERE: I–91 (or I–93) to I–89, northwest to Exit 10; then north on Route 100 to Stowe

The famous Trapp Family Lodge is still credited as the origin of Nordic skiing in America. Its fabled setting—and historical background—make it the best-known touring capital in the East and perhaps the best commercial touring operation in the country.

The well-groomed and well-marked trail system stretches out over 1,700 acres of Green Mountain terrain and offers diversity that ranges from open golf-course terrain to wooded thickets to real wilderness skiing, where it borders on the limitless. Obviously, there is a wide variety of skill levels offered here, and the Trapps provide excellent private or group skiing lessons. The site of many collegiate and world-class races, the lodge also offers racing seminars and backcountry tours.

While there is lodging at the Trapp Family Lodge, it is usually booked months in advance, but there is plenty of lodging throughout Stowe village, along with some extremely precious nightlife. There are weekly races for lodge guests.

STRATTON MOUNTAIN CROSS-COUNTRY CENTER

Stratton Mountain, Vermont 05155
(802) 297–1880 or (802) 297–2200, Extension 2445.

HOURS: 8:30 A.M. to 4:00 P.M.

TRAIL SYSTEM: 32 kilometers (20 miles)

TRAIL DIFFICULTY: Easiest, most difficult

TRAIL GROOMING: Daily, in two areas; skating

RENTAL EQUIPMENT: 160 sets

INSTRUCTION: Yes

FOOD FACILITIES: Tenderloins Restaurant serves lunch and dinner; entertainment on weekends

LODGING: Inns and motels available; call the Stratton reservation service at (802) 222–1300

HOW TO GET THERE: I–91 to Brattleboro, Vermont; northwest on Route 30 to Bondville, then left onto the Stratton Mountain access road

Ski touring at Stratton is like most other things at Stratton, including the Alpine skiing, golf, and tennis: in a word, classy. Stratton is a smooth operation where skiers tour on a smooth and rolling golf course and along wooded trails with pretty views of Stratton Mountain itself and Bromley and Magic mountains. The meandering trails roll through the foothills of the Alpine slopes, some groomed with some others left open.

Stratton's center grooms and tracks 20 miles of trails that take skiers through a variety of experiences, from flat-track running to big rolling heart-stoppers. There are some excellent wilderness trails on the National Forest Terrain—all free. All the rest of Stratton is excellent skiing, well marked and leading to a finely appointed lodge for fire, food, drink, and plenty of talk about the wax you should have used. There are good snacks at the center. By reservation there is a guided tour of Stratton Pond, and throughout the winter there is a cross-country ski festival with plenty of factory vendors and ski reps. Full resort and sports facilities are available nearby.

ROUND BARN FARM

P.O. Box 902
Waitsfield, Vermont 05673
(802) 496–6111

HOURS: 8:30 A.M. to sunset
TRAIL SYSTEM: 30 kilometers (about 18 miles)
TRAIL DIFFICULTY: Mostly intermediate
TRAIL GROOMING: 30 kilometers groomed and trackset
RENTAL EQUIPMENT: Yes
INSTRUCTION: Yes
FOOD FACILITIES: Yes, meals and snacks at the center
LODGING: Rooms for eleven guests
HOW TO GET THERE: Follow Route I-93 to I-89 to Route 100 traveling south to Waitsville, then route 17 to Round Barn Farm

Set in the undulating hills of south-central Vermont, Round Barn Farm is one of those postcard settings in the Green Mountains' maple sugaring country. There is heavy emphasis on grooming here, along with family low-stress skiing. There's not too much in the trail system to baffle the average weekender out for some classic-style striding over rolling farm meadows with wonderful views of the Sugarbush Valley. This is one of those areas that makes a good alternative day to the downhilling in the area (Sugarbush and Mad River Glen). This location also places it within some of the best après ski fare and dining in the state.

TUCKER HILL SKI TOURING CENTER

Tucker Hill Lodge
RFD 1, Box 147
Waitsfield, Vermont 05673
(802) 496–3983, (800) 451–4580

HOURS: 9:00 A.M. to 5:00 P.M.

TRAIL SYSTEM: 45 kilometers (about 27 miles), plus backcountry trails

TRAIL DIFFICULTY: Easiest, more difficult, most difficult

TRAIL GROOMING: Yes, regularly. Some untracked

RENTAL EQUIPMENT: Skis, including Telemark; snowshoes

INSTRUCTION: PSIA-certified

FOOD FACILITIES: Breakfast, lunch, and dinner at Tucker Hill Lodge. Snacks at the touring center

LODGING: Twenty rooms at the Tucker Hill Lodge; also available at Plum Creek

HOW TO GET THERE: I–93 to I–89 to Route 100 south to Waitsfield; then Route 17 heading west to Tucker Hill Lodge, about 2 miles

The Tucker Hill Center is connected to the Sugarbush/Rossignol Ski Touring Center and also the Mad River Nordic Center. The cooperative effort of these areas does much to promote ski touring at a high level; a five-day pass can be obtained to cover the four centers. This southern Vermont area has an extensive, varied, and well-groomed trail network with an emphasis on wooded terrain geared mostly toward the intermediate skier. There's not much here to curl the toes, nor is there much flat-track open terrain for beginners. The trails run over ancient logging roads, and one route leads to the woods-bound Plum Creek, where skiers can find a hot meal and spend the night.

OLE'S CROSS COUNTRY

Airport Road
Warren, Vermont 08674
(802) 496-3430

HOURS: 9:00 A.M. to 5:00 P.M.
TRAIL SYSTEM: 40 kilometers (25 miles)
TRAIL DIFFICULTY: Easiest, more difficult, most difficult
TRAIL GROOMING: More than 20 kilometers
RENTAL EQUIPMENT: Yes
INSTRUCTION: Group and private
FOOD FACILITIES: Cafeteria has hot soups and sandwiches
LODGING: Nearby
HOW TO GET THERE: I–89 north to Exit 3; Route 107 south to Route 100, then north to Warren; right on Brook Road, then left onto Roxbury Gap Road, then left again into Ole's

When the Warren-Sugarbush Airport closes for the winter, that's when Ole Mosesen, a fishing guide from Norway, begins setting tracks throughout the airport terrain—fields and gentle-to-tough woodlands—and gets out the waxes to teach novices what they're about. After his waxing clinics—occasionally involving U.S. Ski Team members—Ole serves a hot lunch to skiers at his cafe. The trail system here is a scenic network through the Mad River Valley with six interconnecting trail loops that range from a 2-mile exercise loop to some heavily pitched verticals for the tough runners. One trail, a 16-kilometer bash through the woods, known as Holly King trail, will leave the most seasoned tourer both exhilarated and beat. Beyond this for the real experts is Scrag Mountain. Full retail and rentals are available.

SUGARBUSH INN CROSS-COUNTRY SKI CENTER

Access Road
Warren, Vermont 05674
(802) 583–2301

HOURS: 9:00 A.M. to 5:00 P.M.

TRAIL SYSTEM: 30 kilometers (about 20 miles)

TRAIL DIFFICULTY: Easiest, more difficult, most difficult

TRAIL GROOMING: Groomed and double trackset daily; skating lanes

RENTAL EQUIPMENT: Yes

INSTRUCTION: Yes

FOOD FACILITIES: Across the street from the touring center at the Sugarbush Inn. Full-service restaurant at the golf course, 1½ miles from the center

LODGING: The inn has forty-six rooms

HOW TO GET THERE: I–93 to I–89 north to Exit 9 at Warren/Waitsfield, Vermont; Route 100 to Warren, then left onto the Sugarbush Valley Access Road; the center is 2 miles on the left

Located in the skirts of the Green Mountains, the Sugarbush/ Rossignol center is a complete, expertly operated and maintained cross-country facility that appeals equally to the racing expert and the recreational skiing family. The center offers 20 kilometers of meticulously groomed and marked trails that vary the experience greatly. You can choose the open-field skiing along the flats of the golf course, or the long, fairly gentle wooded run along German Flats Road to the Tucker Hill Touring Center.

At the touring center, you can sign up for lessons at any level. The center can even arrange a demonstration ride on some Rossignol racing skis for those who want to pursue the go-fast end of the sport. The center has a full retail/rental facility and waxing rooms.

TIMBER CREEK CROSS-COUNTRY SKI CENTER

Box 860
West Dover, Vermont 05356
(802) 464–0999

HOURS: 9:00 A.M. to 4:30 P.M.

TRAIL SYSTEM: 14 kilometers (about 9 miles)

TRAIL DIFFICULTY: Easiest, more difficult, most difficult

TRAIL GROOMING: Groomed and trackset

RENTAL EQUIPMENT: Yes

INSTRUCTION: Yes

FOOD FACILITIES: Restaurant within 1 mile. Light snacks and drinks
  at the center

LODGING: Condominiums at Timber Creek; motels and hotels in the
  area

HOW TO GET THERE: I–91 to Route 9 heading west to Brattleboro;
  west for 20 miles to Wilmington, Vermont; Route 100 for 8 miles
  to Mt. Snow entrance; touring center is across the street

This ski-touring center across from Mt. Snow, with its panoramic
view toward Wilmington Valley, provides for all skiers' needs and
desires. The touring varies from old logging trails across rolling terrain, to open flats and manicured tracks, to skiing in the woolly
wilderness of these parts. There are frozen streams and rivers in the
woods, deep pine groves, and stands of hardwood. Timber Creek
may be small, but it is expanding in its trail-system size. The center
has a full retail and rental operation with a big waxing room. Skiers
who want to try some Telemark turning, or simply Alpine skiing,
can take a free shuttle across to Mt. Snow.

WINDHAM HILL INN
West Townshend, Vermont 05359
(802) 874–4080

HOURS: Dawn to 8:00 P.M.

TRAIL SYSTEM: 8 kilometers (5 miles) of groomed skiing; unlimited wilderness skiing

TRAIL DIFFICULTY: Easiest, more difficult

TRAIL GROOMING: Yes, packed

RENTAL EQUIPMENT: Yes; available free for guests

INSTRUCTION: Yes

FOOD FACILITIES: Meal service for guests of the inn

LODGING: Fifteen guest rooms with private baths

HOW TO GET THERE: I–91 to Exit 2 and Brattleboro, Vermont; Route 30 north for 22 miles to West Townshend and Windham Hill

This restored nineteenth-century family farmhouse in southern Vermont is a lovely setting for destination skiers who like primarily wilderness skiing over meadows and through woods. The inn itself, run by Grigs and Pat Markham, offers full amenities for most skiers' tastes, and more: It is rich in antiques and Oriental rugs, handmade quilts, and original paintings—the charms of a past age. The skiing facility is for the exclusive use of guests. There are no trail fees nor any charge for equipment use. Aside from its own small groomed network, Windham Hill has wild open lands, mostly of the gentle-contour variety. This skiing feeds onto other trail systems like Tater Hill, Viking, Stratton, and Wild Wings. Trails are for guests only.

CATAMOUNT FAMILY CENTER

421 Governor Chittenden Road
Williston, Vermont 05495
(802) 879–6001

HOURS: Sunday, Monday, and Tuesday, 9:00 A.M. to dusk; Wednesday through Saturday, 9:00 A.M. to 9:00 P.M.

TRAIL SYSTEM: 40 kilometers (25 miles)

TRAIL DIFFICULTY: Easiest, more difficult, most difficult

TRAIL GROOMING: More than 30 kilometers as needed, single track-set; skating lanes

RENTAL EQUIPMENT: 70 sets

INSTRUCTION: PSIA-certified

FOOD FACILITIES: Hot drinks and trail snacks at the center; restaurants available within 3 miles

LODGING: Bed-and-breakfast inns and hotels within 2 miles; Burlington, Vermont, is 8 miles away

HOW TO GET THERE: I–93 to I–89 to Vermont Exit 12, then north; right at the second traffic light; 4 miles to the center

This fifth-generation family farm outside Burlington typifies the kind of old-world solid roots at the center of much of Vermont's charm. The well-groomed and well-marked trail system makes gentle loops over fields and woods in the Champlain Valley and offers wonderful sudden views of Camel's Hump and Mt. Mansfield. Though the grade varies just 300 feet vertically throughout the network, there are still a few huff-and-puffers like Ridge Run and Skidway that throw you twisting, quick descents. There are heated trail shelters out on the loop. At night, 3 kilometers are lit for running. The center is in a circa 1796 farmhouse. The area always features snowshoeing and ice skating.

HERMITAGE CROSS-COUNTRY TOURING CENTER

Coldbrook Road
Wilmington, Vermont 05363
(802) 464-3511

HOURS: 9:00 A.M. to 4:00 P.M.

TRAIL SYSTEM: 50 kilometers (about 31 miles)

TRAIL DIFFICULTY: Easiest, more difficult, most difficult. Telemark trails

TRAIL GROOMING: Most trails, as needed

RENTAL EQUIPMENT: Yes

INSTRUCTION: Yes

FOOD FACILITIES: Full meals and trail snacks

LODGING: At the inn (twenty-nine rooms)

HOW TO GET THERE: I-91 to Brattleboro, Vermont; west on Route 9 to Wilmington

Two thousand feet up in the Vermont sky, The Hermitage has plenty of snow and touring, generally in woods and stream beds sheltered from the wind. The Ridge Trails run from the top of Haystack Ski Area to the top of Mt. Snow, a 5-mile trek through the National Forest. This is a special springtime challenge for expert skiers and must be guided. In March there are several challenge races at the area as well. There is also good beginner skiing along the flat floor of the Mt. Snow Valley, and intermediates can climb up along the shoulders of the mountains. Like so many Vermont inns, the Hermitage is reconstructed from an eighteenth-century farmhouse and offers the kind of quaint charm tourers look for in such places. The 50 kilometers of marked and groomed trails circle from the inn out to Mt. Snow. The touring center offers full retail and rental services and trail snacks including wine and cheese.

INN AT QUAIL RUN

Smith Road
Wilmington, Vermont 05363
(802) 464–3362

HOURS: Daylight

TRAIL SYSTEM: Inn at Quail Run is tied in with the Sitzmark Ski Touring Center with its 35 kilometers (about 21 miles) of trails. Total network is 50 kilometers (about 30 miles)

TRAIL DIFFICULTY: More difficult

TRAIL GROOMING: Packed and trackset as needed

RENTAL EQUIPMENT: Nearby

INSTRUCTION: Nearby

FOOD FACILITIES: Gourmet cuisine for lodge guests; full bar and lodge facility for guests

LODGING: Contemporary rooms with private baths available

HOW TO GET THERE: I–91 from Brattleboro, Vermont; Route 9 west to Wilmington; then Route 100 north for 4 miles to the town center

This is a small inn straight out of a romantic novel. It sits nearly 2,000 feet up in the southern Green Mountains with some terrific views of this rolling range and of peaks such as Mt. Snow and Haystack. These latter locations are full-blown Alpine areas. Cross-country skiers have 30 miles of private trails at their disposal, all of them starting at the door of the inn. Skiing is for Inn guests only. There are plenty of flats for beginners to get their ski legs and the well seasoned to do some warm-up runs before plunging into the special Wilderness trail that runs through snow-coated woodlands, cellar holes filled with rich history, and ponds with beaver lodges and other wildlife—even some beech trees with bear claw marks scratched in the side. If, after the long wilderness tour or the run through the flattish meadows, skiers have anything left in them, the area is near the rollicking Mt. Snow with its celebrated nightlife. This can be embraced or avoided, as skiers wish.

SITZMARK LODGE
Wilmington, Vermont 05363
(802) 464–5498

HOURS: 9:00 A.M. to 5:00 P.M

TRAIL SYSTEM: 35 kilometers (about 22 miles)

TRAIL DIFFICULTY: Easiest, more difficult, most difficult

TRAIL GROOMING: Groomed daily, with 6 kilometers of skating lanes

RENTAL EQUIPMENT: Yes

INSTRUCTION: PSIA-certified

FOOD FACILITIES: Meals served at The Barn Lounge, weekends and holidays

LODGING: Inns and hotels in the area

HOW TO GET THERE: I–91 to Brattleboro, Vermont; Route 9 heading west to Wilmington; 4 miles north on Route 100 to Sitzmark

Cross-country skiers at Sitzmark enjoy some spectacular views of the Mt. Snow and Haystack mountain range to the west of the center, as they glide over a wide variety of trails. From the slow rollers, to choppers such as Ponderosa View, this trail system offers something to all levels. Advanced skiers can climb into some stunning mountain plateaus surrounding the center, while novice skiers get their training on an 18-hole golf course and attendant pasture trails. Sitzmark trails are also used by Quail Run guests.

THE WHITE HOUSE OF WILMINGTON

Route 9, P.O. Box 757
Wilmington, Vermont 05363
(802) 464-2136

HOURS: 9:00 A.M. to 4:30 P.M.

TRAIL SYSTEM: 45 kilometers (about 27 miles)

TRAIL DIFFICULTY: Easiest, more difficult, most difficult

TRAIL GROOMING: Consistently over 30 kilometers

RENTAL EQUIPMENT: 100 sets

INSTRUCTION: Video lessons available

FOOD FACILITIES: Continental dining at the White House plus skiers' lunches on weekends. Open to the public

LODGING: Twelve rooms at the White House

HOW TO GET THERE: I-91 to Brattleboro, Vermont; Route 9 west to Wilmington and junction of Route 100

The White House itself, set in the Mt. Snow region, is a turn-of-the-century mansion steeped in Vermont's rural hospitality. With full health spa, sauna, and indoor pool available, and truly exquisite continental cuisine served before roaring fires, this is a place to come home to after a day on the trail. Eight rooms are in the main inn, and four are in the north wing.

The trails are skewed toward intermediates, but there is plenty for the novice and expert as well. Skiing begins with undulating meadow skiing over nicely groomed tracks and progresses to toe-curling downhills over the twisting Raponda Primitive Trail. Not for everyone, this is nevertheless a special run feeding into the Ridge Trail that goes between Haystack and Mt. Snow and offers wonderful vistas of each.

HILLTOP CROSS-COUNTRY CENTER

Box 2820
Wolcott, Vermont 05680
(802) 888–3710

HOURS: Saturdays, Sundays, and holidays from 9:00 A.M. to 5:00 P.M.
TRAIL SYSTEM: 20 kilometers (about 12 miles)
TRAIL DIFFICULTY: Easiest, more difficult, most difficult
TRAIL GROOMING: Yes
RENTAL EQUIPMENT: Yes
INSTRUCTION: No
FOOD FACILITIES: None at the center; restaurant within 3 miles
LODGING: Within 5 miles
HOW TO GET THERE: Route I–92 to I–89 to Route 15

This small area north of Stowe Village offers good skiing, mostly of the gentle meadow variety, though there is one cranker that sends skiers twisting up and down through the woods. It is very much a locals' area or perhaps a day trip off the beaten path for visitors at Stowe who want to escape the crush. Though the facilities are not for most destination skiiers, this is still the luscious land area of northern Vermont, and the trails are an excellent combination of old logging roads and open flats.

WOODSTOCK SKI TOURING CENTER

At the Woodstock Country Club
Route 106
Woodstock, Vermont 05091
(802) 457–6674, (800) 448–7900

HOURS: 9:00 A.M. to dusk
TRAIL SYSTEM: 61 kilometers (about 37 miles)
TRAIL DIFFICULTY: Least difficult, more difficult, most difficult
TRAIL GROOMING: 61 kilometers groomed and double-trackset, or
groomed for skating, daily
RENTAL EQUIPMENT: Yes

INSTRUCTION: PSIA-certified

FOOD FACILITIES: Restaurant and bar at the center and at the Woodstock Inn; indoor sports center 1 mile from center.

LODGING: Inns and motels in the region

HOW TO GET THERE: I–91 to I–89; west to Route 4; west to Route 106; then south to the touring center

In the heart of this most tweedy Rock Resort (for owner Laurance Rockefeller) town of Woodstock, Vermont—where skiing all got organized in America some five decades ago under the agreeable patriarchy of Dartmouth College—this touring area offers an extensive trail system to skiers who can do without roughing it or the "wilderness experience." It is rather tuned to those vacationers seeking the pleasures of ski touring within the resort experience. Woodstock itself, with the famous inn at its center, is considered by many one of the loveliest towns in New England.

Both skating and classic tracks are maintained on the trails, one loop winds along century-old carriage roads through a Vermont tree farm with openings, and overlooks the serene countryside. Some land previously in the Rockefeller estate is now maintained by the park service. Other trails wind up Mt. Tom and Mt. Peg, and there are flatter trials as well for golf course and woods skiing.

The Touring Center offers one of the most extensive base facilities in New England. It is wonderfully large and replete with a big, steamy shower room, rental shop, ski shop, restaurant, lounge with fireplace, and a large waxing porch. For skiers in fear of overexpending their energy, there is one trail loop that brings you mercifully close to the back door of the Woodstock Inn. Here, for a mere pittance, you can park your skis and start a hot and huge brunch with salmon bisque against a background of Mozart études.

NEW HAMPSHIRE

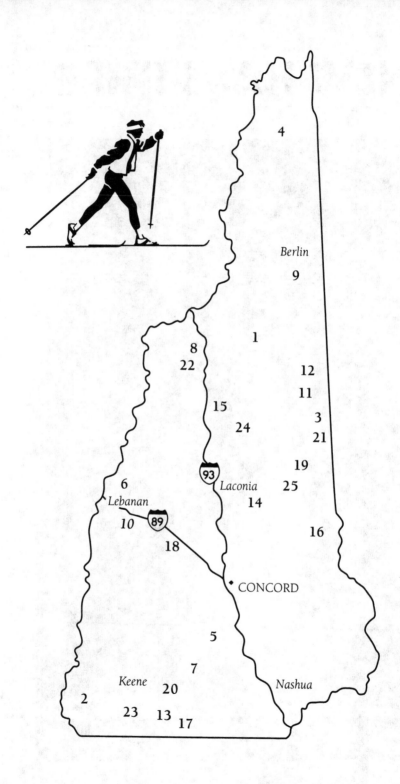

NEW HAMPSHIRE

Numbers on map refer to towns numbered below

BRETTON WOODS CROSS-COUNTRY SKI CENTER

Bretton Woods, New Hampshire 03575
(603) 278–5181

HOURS: 8:30 A.M. to 4:30 P.M.

TRAIL SYSTEM: 90 kilometers (about 54 miles)

TRAIL DIFFCULTY: Least difficult, more difficult, most difficult

TRAIL GROOMING: Single track with skating lanes on half the trail system

RENTAL EQUIPMENT: Yes

INSTRUCTION: PSIA-certified

FOOD FACILITIES: Food and drink available at the Touring Center cafeteria, Alpine base lodge, Darby's Tavern, and Fabyan's

LODGING: At the Bretton Woods Lodge or Rosebrook Townhouses near the Touring Center. Lodging for 800.

HOW TO GET THERE: I–93 to Lincoln, New Hampshire; bear right on Route 3 to Twin Mountain, then right on Route 302 at light; the center is 4 miles on the left, across from the Alpine area

Coursing through the western valley of Mt. Washington, this spectacular, 90-kilometer trail system is truly all things for all skiers, from the raw neophyte seeking a leisurely walk through the White Mountain National Forest, to the serious racer looking to train on tracks graced in the past by such world-class runners as Bill Koch, Tim and Jennifer Caldwell, and Beth Paxson. The U.S. Team held its 1982 Nationals here, and the area hosts an annual stop on the Great American Ski Chase marathon series.

Do no be scared off by all this heaviness, however. Bretton Woods's bread and butter is still the casual touring skier, and the area gears itself to just that. A very well marked trail system offers courses of various lengths and degrees of difficulty, from the broad flats of the golf course on which is located that gorgeous antique, the Mt. Washington Hotel, to the Coronary Hill system, which winds into foothills of the Presidential Range. There are three separate but interlocking trail systems at Bretton Woods—the Ammonoosuc, Deception (for Mount Deception), and Stickney—the latter incorporating the Alpine area and offering the most hilly and tough terrain. You'll do well to stay away from the Cog Railway Road since this is a major snowmobile route.

Bretton Woods has lately moved its touring center into a much larger building with full and very well appointed accommodations—a large restaurant and waxing room, a full rental operation, a ski school, and some just-hanging-around space to let skiers thaw the ice out of their beards.

Though skiers can jump on trails from the roadside anywhere around the White Mountain National Forest here, this is not advised for folks unfamiliar with the area. It is vast. The trail system is bewildering. Part of the trail fee pays for the plasticized maps you pick up at the touring center, which offer advice about shelters along the trail and the level of difficulty for the various routes. The area is on the opposite side of Mt. Washington from Jackson, and as the sun sets on a winter afternoon, the mountain holds the light longer in the sky as it blinks through the spectrum—orange to red to violet to blue. If Jackson is the place to watch the winter sunrise, then Bretton Woods is the spot to view amazing sunsets. Overnight and moonlight excursions are available.

The area has a limited number of beds at this point—less than one hundred—including existing Rosebrook townhouses and The Lodge motel, but motels are available down Route 302 toward Twin Mountain.

ROAD'S END FARM

Jackson Hill Road
Chesterfield, New Hampshire 03443
(603) 363-4703

HOURS: 9:00 A.M. to 5:00 P.M.

TRAIL SYSTEM: 32 kilometers (about 19 miles)

TRAIL DIFFICULTY: Easiest, more difficult, most difficult

TRAIL GROOMING: Trackset

RENTAL EQUIPMENT: Yes

INSTRUCTION: Weekends, holidays, and school vacations

FOOD FACILITIES: Sandwiches, soup, and snacks available on weekends, holidays, and vacations

LODGING: Inns and motels in the area, and at the farm. Lots of housing (1,500 beds) within 10 miles of area

HOW TO GET THERE: I-91 north to Exit 3 at Brattleboro, Vermont; then Route 9E to junction of Route 63; south on Route 63 to center of Chesterfield; turn left for 1 mile to Jackson Hill Road; follow to the touring center.

Here is a Revolutionary War farmstead in the gently rolling landscape near Mt. Monadnock that has served as equestrian land for nearly thirty years. Ezra Jackson was a homsteader on this 600-acre tract in 1778. At first snowfall the bridle paths are instantly transformed into cross-country trails that are well conceived and cared for. The ski terrain varies from open meadows to deep wooded forests and sudden clearings that look out over the Green Mountains of southern Vermont: Monadnock, Ascutney, Stratton, Bromley, Haystack, Snow, and Lake Spofford—a 40-mile vista. After the 30 kilometers are exhausted—rather impossible even in a season of regular visits—skiers can access the large forests of the 12,000-acre Pisgah Wilderness Area, a region where ungroomed logging trails and paths course endlessly. Rentals are available at Road's End Farm, as well as informal instruction by appointment.

THE DARBY FIELD INN
Box D, Bald Hill
Conway, New Hampshire 03818
(603) 447–2181

HOURS: 8:00 A.M. to 4:00 P.M.; for guests of the inn only

TRAIL SYSTEM: 15 kilometers (about 9 miles)

TRAIL DIFFICULTY: Easiest, more difficult, most difficult

TRAIL GROOMING: Yes

RENTAL EQUIPMENT: No

INSTRUCTION: No

FOOD FACILITIES: Dining room for breakfast and dinner. Dinner open to public

LODGING: Seventeen rooms in the inn

HOW TO GET THERE: I-93 to Exit 24; Route 3 north to Route 25, northeast to Route 16; north to Bald Hill

The top of Bald Hill provides an eagle's eye panorama of the Mountain Washington Valley and the whole Presidential Range. The scenery is as stunning as any you'll find in New England ski country, and the setting is an inn converted from a big farmhouse—now offering seventeen bedrooms. From quaint Victorian interiors to the breadth of the New Hampshire mountain sky, the Darby Field Inn is a good choice for nearly any touring skier. After a day of tough running or just leisurely plodding through woods, the sunset view of the valley from the dining room is an amazing delight.

The trails themselves have a nice variety; they are only partially groomed and tracked and draw skiers through hilly, wooded terrain. Skiers wanting more terrain can easily jump into the White Mountain National Forest, less than 1 mile from the takeoff point at the inn. Equipment rentals, instruction, waxing advice, and the like are not available at the inn, but the ski town of North Conway is just a few miles away.

THE BALSAMS WILDERNESS

Dixville Notch, New Hampshire 03576
(603) 255-3400, (800) 255-0600 (continental U.S.),
(800) 255-0800 (N.H.)

HOURS: 8:30 A.M. to 4:00 P.M.

TRAIL SYSTEM: 75 kilometers (45 miles)

TRAIL DIFFICULTY: Easiest, more difficult, most difficult

TRAIL GROOMING: Double trackset by machine, skating

RENTAL EQUIPMENT: Cross-country and Telemark. Some skating

INSTRUCTION: Yes

FOOD FACILITIES: Dining at the Balsams. Cafeteria at ski area

LODGING: More than 230 rooms in the Grand Balsams Resort Hotel

HOW TO GET THERE: I-93 to Lincoln, New Hampshire; Route 3 to Colebrook, and east on Route 26 to Dixville Notch. Alternate route from Boston: I-95 to Portsmouth; Route 16 to Route 26; west to Dixville Notch

As a downhill area, the Balsams Wilderness "estate" has gained a reputation as one of the most pampering ski experiences in New England, and that holds for cross-country aficionados as well. Else-

where, we have discussed the advantages of a cross-country area that can share the amenities and atmosphere of an established downhill area on the same premises—restaurants, lodges, housing, and the trail system, to name a few. For diners the gourmet experience at the Balsams is not one to be taken lightly, no matter what your ski preference. The Grand Balsams Resort Hotel has more than 230 rooms, and the management does not care if your skis are skinny, wide, or a little of each. Rental and retail gear is available for both Alpine and Nordic.

That said, the touring experience can certainly stand on its own merits here. The trail system is set in the fortress wall of the White Mountains entrance of Dixville Notch. There is wonderful scenic wilderness throughout the region, both on the well-groomed trackset trails and the outback wilderness trails that meander across the estate.

COUNTRYSIDE CROSS-COUNTRY SKI CENTER

Route 13
Dunbarton, New Hampshire 03045
(603) 774–5031

HOURS: 9:00 A.M. to dusk, Wednesday through Sunday

TRAIL SYSTEM: 20 kilometers (about 12 miles)

TRAIL DIFFICULTY: Easiest, more difficult

TRAIL GROOMING: Yes; tracks with skating lanes

RENTAL EQUIPMENT: Yes

INSTRUCTION: Yes

FOOD FACILITIES: Restaurant at the clubhouse

LODGING: Several inns and motels within 8 miles of the center

HOW TO GET THERE: I–93 to Route 101; turn onto Route 114 in Goffs-town and follow Route 13 North for 5½ miles to the country club

Valley View Country Club is a fine example of good ski touring on golf-course terrain and surrounding open countryside. It is a day-tripper's area, encompassing open-field, trackset skiing with some off-the-trail powder-breaking as well. This area operates at a leisurely pace, and novices can benefit in a low-pressure environment from a good instruction and gentle terrain. The trails around the pond are open and wooded.

MOOSE MOUNTAIN LODGE

Box 272
Etna, New Hampshire 03750
(603) 643–3529

HOURS: Daylight

TRAIL SYSTEM: 50 kilometers (30 miles); ungroomed backcountry for guests only

TRAIL DIFFICULTY: Easiest, more difficult, most difficult

TRAIL GROOMING: No

RENTAL EQUIPMENT: Yes, for guests

INSTRUCTION: Informal teaching is included with the lodge stay

FOOD FACILITIES: For guests only, three meals daily

LODGING: Twelve guest rooms

HOW TO GET THERE: I–89 to Exit 18; north on Route 120 for ½ mile to a right turn on Etna Road; turn right again ½ mile beyond the Etna Store onto Rudsboro Road; then 2 miles to a left turn onto Dana Road. Go ½ mile, then turn right up hill. **Caution:** At times this is tricky terrain to negotiate by car. Please call ahead.

Once an Alpine area in the formative days of the sport (the 1930s), Moose Mountain was converted into a ski-touring center that commands the lovely sweep of the Green Mountains and the Connecticut River Valley. Ghosts of those pioneer skiers seem still with the place, though now Kay and Peter Shumway operate the area solely as an inn, with ski touring a feature attraction for guests only. The area lacks public facilities, and at times the steep ascent up Moose Mountain is accessible only to overland vehicles. The area features a trail system that begins uphill at the front door of the inn. Skiers skim quickly into the fir woodlands and then run down through exhilarating chutes out into dazzling open meadows. Here, the Appalachian Trail crosses, and skiers can use the many trails established by the Dartmouth Outing Club. The interior of the lodge is ideal for folks who have long since traded in the crowded nightlife for lingering home-cooked meals in front of radiant stone fireplaces.

TORY PINES

Route 47
Francestown, New Hampshire 03043
(603) 588–2000

HOURS: 9:00 A.M. to 4:30 P.M.

TRAIL SYSTEM: 13 kilometers (about 8 miles); combined with Crotched Mountain trails

TRAIL DIFFICULTY: Easiest, more difficult, most difficult

TRAIL GROOMING: Daily

RENTAL EQUIPMENT: 100 sets

INSTRUCTION: Yes

FOOD FACILITIES: Restaurant in the center of trail system

LODGING: Twenty-eight rooms in the hotel; another hotel $1/10$ mile away

HOW TO GET THERE: Take I–91 to Brattleboro, Vermont; Route 9 east to Keene, New Hampshire; Route 101 east to Route 202; north on Route 202 to Route 47 and then east to Tory Pines

Tory Pines combined efforts with Crotched Mountain to operate a 50-kilometer groomed, trackset, marked, and patrolled trail system. This boosts the Tory Pine traditional system by about 20 kilometers and opens the ski terrain into some hilly challenges and real cruising destinations for lunchtime stops. The areas combine their efforts also on the purchase of rental equipment, retail gear, and instruction—including Telemarking, which makes use of Crotched's downhill slopes. There is special attention here to beginners, who can purchase attractive lesson/rental/trail-pass packages. Night skiing and Alpine are also available.

Tory itself is a 400-acre spread at the foot of Crotched and offers skiing over open golf-course terrain and through dense woods that open suddenly into spectacular views of the Monadnock region of lakes and mountains. All trails seem to lead eventually to a wonderful Revolutionary-period tavern, the Snooty Fox, which features fireside wine sipping and gourmet cuisine.

CANNON MOUNTAIN

Franconia, New Hampshire 03580
(603) 823–5563

HOURS: 8:00 A.M. to 4:30 P.M., at Alpine area with access to cross-country trails

TRAIL SYSTEM: 8 kilometers (5 miles); bike paths good for skiing when snow-covered

TRAIL DIFFICULTY: Easiest, more difficult

TRAIL GROOMING: None

RENTAL EQUIPMENT: Yes, in nearby shop

INSTRUCTION: No

FOOD FACILITIES: Restaurants nearby; a snack bar and cafeteria at the mountain

LODGING: Motels and inns in the region

HOW TO GET THERE: I–93 to Lincoln, then north on Route 3 through Franconia Notch to Exit 1, Flume Visitors' Center for bikepaths; Exit 3 for Echo Lake Parking Lot

Cannon is one of the woolliest of the old-time ski areas. It was hewn out of the rugged granite uplands back in the skimeister days of the 1930s before disciplines were so specialized. Thus, it is possible that members of the Nansen Ski Club, the first ski-touring organization in the nation, skinned their way up Cannon and jumped off the edge of the earth for a shot down the Taft Highway. These days, of course, there is a full, smallish, Nordic trail system as well as the Alpine area of Cannon. The Nordic area is rather casual, but pretty. Nordic skiers leave from the Echo Lake parking lot at Franconia Notch State Park and run in the woodlands at the base of these granite towers. The trail system is within the state park.

FRANCONIA INN CROSS-COUNTRY SKI AREA

Route 116, Easton Road
Franconia, New Hampshire 03580
(603) 823–5542 or 1–800–RELAXX

HOURS: 9:00 A.M. to 5:00 P.M.

TRAIL SYSTEM: 60 kilometers (about 38 miles)

TRAIL DIFFICULTY: Easiest, more difficult, most difficult

TRAIL GROOMING: All groomed and trackset

RENTAL EQUIPMENT: Yes

INSTRUCTION: Yes

FOOD FACILITIES: Restaurant at inn

LODGING: Rooms available at inn

HOW TO GET THERE: I–93 to Franconia; Exit 38, south on Route 116, then 2½ miles to Inn on right

Located in one of the historic mountain settings of the Northeast, this ski area offers a view of the notch, of the Kinsman Range, of Mt. Lafayette, and the entire eastern valley of the White Mountain Range. It is land steeped in outdoor history. It is also quite demanding in spots, groomed with a lovely touch, and easily accessible from Boston. The trail system itself, spread out through the granite knobs and fir-forest-terrain of the region, is a healthy 38 miles and ranges from gently sloped meadows to high shoulder skiing. With the number of motels, inns, and restaurants surrounding this trail system, it is fun to make a loop of many days. Maps are available showing you just how to do this.

Franconia Inn itself is a pleasant facility, and the barn beside it is a good retail shop for waxes and gear, instruction, contacts with guides, and box lunches for the trail. The inn is a fine destination for skiers who want to keep coming back.

AMC PINKHAM NOTCH CAMP

Box 298
Gorham, New Hampshire 03581
(603) 466–2725

HOURS: Daylight

TRAIL SYSTEM: 50 kilometers (about 31 miles)

TRAIL DIFFICULTY: Easiest, more difficult, most difficult

TRAIL GROOMING: None

RENTAL EQUIPMENT: None

INSTRUCTION: No formal program

FOOD FACILITIES: Breakfast and dinner at base camp; reservations required for dinner. Trail lunches available if ordered the night before. Buffet lunches on weekends

LODGING: Capacity for more than 100 persons; reservations advised. Dormitory-style bunking; shared baths

HOW TO GET THERE: I–95 to the Spaulding Turnpike to Route 16. Camp is 17 miles north of North Conway.

The AMC Camp at Pinkham Notch, the base of Mt. Washington, is one of the original outback mountaineering camps in New England. It is for the serious of purpose, the skillful, the experienced skier. That said, Pinkham Notch Camp also provides some of the greatest wilderness skiing anywhere. In places the trails are tied in with the Jackson Ski Touring facility, which is of similar stripe. Along with individual skiing, there are several programs available, including weekend workshops, winter camping and snowshoeing, Telemarking, and photography. There are also evening programs and lectures.

Located at the eastern base of Mt. Washington in the heart of the White Mountain National Forest, the Pinkham Camp opens onto the rolling terrain of the shoulders of the Presidential Range, including the downhill area of Wildcat. This is some of the most breathtaking scenery in the Northeast, and there are several choices. One stimulating 6-miler is the Avalanche Brook Ski Trail, connecting Pinkham Notch Camp with the Dana Place Inn to the south. This trail climbs nearly 1,000 feet, then drops 1,500 feet through fir and hardwood thicket. You'll cross bridges over streams, then end with a 1-mile run over Rocky Branch Trail and a meadow surrounding the Dana Place Inn.

This is one of the typical Pinkham Camp trails, and the most adventurous can pick up the trail from Jackson on this route. Described as "challenging skiing," that really means knowing what you're about. Don't attempt it alone or in bad skiing conditions. On the other hand, the reward of such a trail is some of the most exhilarating skiing in New England.

GREAT GLEN TRAILS

P.O. Box 300
Gorham, New Hampshire 03581
(603) 466–2333

HOURS: 9:00 A.M. to 4:30 P.M.

TRAIL SYSTEM: 19 kilometers (about 12 miles)

TRAIL DIFFICULTY: Easiest, more difficult

TRAIL GROOMING: More than 19 kilometers

RENTAL EQUIPMENT: Yes

INSTRUCTION: Yes

FOOD FACILITIES: Yes cafeteria dining

LODGING: Several inns and motels in the region

HOW TO GET THERE: Follow Route 93 to Exit 35, then Route 3 traveling north to route 115 north, to Route 2 east, to Route 16 south to the Mount Washington Autoroad

On site of the Northern Presidentials, Great Glen Trails makes use of Mt. Washington, yet is to be clearly separated from Washington's fierce reputation for danger and killer cold weather. Rather, the skiing at Great Glen speaks more of fine grooming in the rolling terrain bordering the northern Presidential Range. Great Gulf Wilderness is a federally designated wild area (no development), and has always been considered one of the jewels of this countryside, from both a recreational and aesthetic viewpoint. Skiers can access backcountry terrain off the trail, and can also ride a fourteen-passenger snow cat 4 miles up the Autoroad for a long easy descent from the 4,000-foot mark back to the center. For aficionados of the sport, one of the exciting possibilities in the future of this new area is a tie in with Jackson some 12 miles to the south.

EASTMAN SKI TOURING CENTER

Box 53
Grantham, New Hampshire 03753
(603) 863–4500

HOURS: 9:00 A.M. to 4:00 P.M.

TRAIL SYSTEM: 30 kilometers (about 19 miles)

TRAIL DIFFICULTY: Easiest, more difficult, most difficult

TRAIL GROOMING: Groomed and double trackset

RENTAL EQUIPMENT: 95 sets

INSTRUCTION: Group and semiprivate lessons including Telemark and skating clinics

FOOD FACILITIES: Harvey's Restaurant at the center serves drinks and lunch

LODGING: Inns and motels in the area

HOW TO GET THERE: I–93 to I–89 north at Bow, New Hampshire, to Exit 13 at Grantham; turn right; the Eastman road is less than a ½ mile on the right

Eastman is a lovely four-season vacation resort spread out in the pine valley of the Sugar River in the west-central region of the state. The well-marked and well-cared-for trail system encompasses all the features of the resort: golf course, woods, rolling hills including a small Alpine slope, and stream beds that feed into Eastman Pond. Novice skiers can work on the relative flats of Lazy Loop around the golf course, and as they get adventurous, work out into the woods loops. The 5-kilometer Deerpath Loop will test anyone's skills, and for distance, skirting Eastman Pond can be close to a 9-kilometer project. The countryside is pretty, with views of the surrounding mountains, and the amenities at the center are complete: rental and retail shop, waxing area, and ready instruction. At the center, Harvey's is a good-sized lounge that serves drinks and a limited lunch menu.

MOUNT WASHINGTON VALLEY

P.O. Box 646
Intervale, New Hampshire 03845
(603) 356–3113

HOURS: 9:00 A.M. to 5:00 P.M., December 1 to March 30

TRAIL SYSTEM: 35 kilometers (about 22 miles) of groomed trail with 70 kilometers (about 43 miles) overall

TRAIL DIFFICULTY: Easiest, more difficult, most difficult

TRAIL GROOMING: Trackset over 60 kilometers

RENTAL EQUIPMENT: 200 sets

INSTRUCTION: PSIA-certified ski school

FOOD FACILITIES: Several nearby restaurants and three inns

LODGING: Country inns and motor lodges

HOW TO GET THERE: I–93 to Exit 24; Route 3 north to Route 25; northeast to Route 16, north through Conway and North Conway; then Route 16A 3 miles to the center

Located in Intervale, Mount Washington Valley is dedicated to the proposition that skiers at any level can learn a thing or twenty about the sport. The instructors are as fun as they are effective and will eventually want to work you out on the hillside. The trails are well marked and groomed, most of them offering nice views of Mt. Washington and the Moat Range. Skiers will use many of the old logging roads that crisscross the region, and some may opt to climb the saddle of Bartlett Mountain with its scenic overlooks. Several moonlight and cookout tours are available through the season.

JACKSON SKI TOURING FOUNDATION

Box 216
Jackson, New Hampshire 03846
(800) XC-SNOWS

HOURS: 8:00 A.M. to 5:30 P.M.

TRAIL SYSTEM: 160 kilometers (103 miles)

TRAIL DIFFICULTY: Easiest, more difficult, most difficult

TRAIL GROOMING: 60 kilometers groomed daily; 45 kilometers for skating
RENTAL EQUIPMENT: Yes
INSTRUCTION: Yes
FOOD FACILITIES: Several nearby restaurants
LODGING: Several inns and motels in the area
HOW TO GET THERE: I–95 to Spaulding Turnpike; Route 16N to Jackson; center is in middle of village

Aside from its legendary stature as the historic capital of cross-country skiing, and with plenty of echoes of the skimeister days when it took all morning to "skin" up Black Mountain for one run down, the village of Jackson is simply astoundingly beautiful. Classic New England is what you get here, from the old covered bridge that welcomes you into town to the white church in the center of the village, and the exciting pace of serious ski touring—all under the command of Mt. Washington.

Do not be deterred by the talk of serious skiing, however. True, from start to finish Jackson exudes the sport. But still, there's plenty here for the novice, the snowshoer, the hiker, or the vacationer simply looking for delicious mountain experience.

Jackson truly goes to the roots of the region. It is a non-profit operation that combines the efforts of the U.S. Forest Service and several private landowners. Since the 1970s it has been incorporated for the sole purpose of advancing cross-country skiing. Of the 152 kilometers of trails, 60 are groomed carefully, and often. Skiers wind through hardwood forest land, open-gladed meadows, and upland wilderness that leads into the shoulders of the Presidential Range. Across the river and into the trees, the Ellis River Trail winds in a long, slightly uphill loop along the river to a woodland inn; the way home is an easy downhill breezer all the way back to the road. For off-track skiers there is ample opportunity for backpacking and camping trips into the backlands on mountain skis.

At the Jackson Ski Touring Foundation building you will find the Jack Frost Ski Shop, which will rent or sell equipment and all kinds of retail accessories. Here you can sign up for a lesson, take a waxing clinic, or sign up for a night-skiing foray. And, finally, for the inexhaustible, Jackson and its environs has a full lineup of terrific nightlife.

SHATTUCK INN NORDIC SKI CENTER
Jaffrey, New Hampshire 03452
(603) 532–4300

HOURS: 9:00 A.M. to 4:30 P.M.

TRAIL SYSTEM: 13 kilometers (about 9 miles)

TRAIL DIFFICULTY: Easiest, more difficult

TRAIL GROOMING: All groomed and trackset

RENTAL EQUIPMENT: Yes

INSTRUCTION: No

FOOD FACILITIES: Snack bar

LODGING: Inns in the area

HOW TO GET THERE: From Nashua take Route 101 heading west to Peterboro, then south on Route 202 to Jaffrey Center

When the winter sends southern New Hampshire her fair share of snowfall, Shattuck becomes one of those golf course ski areas that gets transformed into deep winter. On the course itself, the skiing is confined to the cart paths that branch throughout the eighteen holes. This is lovely skiing at the base of Mt. Monadnock.

WOODBOUND INN

Jaffrey, New Hampshire 03452
(603) 532–8341

HOURS: 9:00 A.M. to 5:00 P.M.
TRAIL SYSTEM: 36 kilometers (about 22 miles)
TRAIL DIFFICULTY: Easiest, more difficult, most difficult
TRAIL GROOMING: As needed
RENTAL EQUIPMENT: Yes
INSTRUCTION: Yes
FOOD FACILITIES: Restaurant at the inn, serving all three meals
LODGING: Forty-two rooms and cottages at the inn
HOW TO GET THERE: Route 2 in Massachusetts to Route 202, then north into New Hampshire and to Woodbound

With 36 kilometers of nicely set tracks opening into the state forest land—not to mention a downhill practice slope for Telemark work—Woodbound has a total ski experience to offer its guest. The trail system varies from gently rolling flattish land, with running tracks, to wilderness shots up, down, and all around through the public lands.

In addition, Woodbound offers the extras for everyone to enjoy all the little corners of winter—from night tobogganing down specially sculpted chutes, to ice skating and sleigh rides, then indoors for movies. The food is homemade and renowned in ski country.

GUNSTOCK CROSS-COUNTRY CENTER
Box 1307
Laconia, New Hampshire 03247
(603) 293–4341

HOURS: 8:30 A.M. to 4:00 P.M.

TRAIL SYSTEM: 32 kilometers (about 21 miles)

TRAIL DIFFICULTY: Easiest, more difficult, most difficult

TRAIL GROOMING: Double trackset daily, skating lanes

RENTAL EQUIPMENT: 100 sets

INSTRUCTION: All ability levels, including Telemark

FOOD FACILITIES: Cafeteria in the main ski lodge; soup, sandwiches, and snacks

LODGING: Several motels and inns nearby

HOW TO GET THERE: I–93 to Exit 20; Route 3 to Route 11A; follow to Gunstock

With its 5-kilometer zinger, where several U.S. Nordic Combined championships have been held, to its gentle trails that wind the novice skier through some lovely winter woods, Gunstock offers the entire spectrum of the sport. And as with many Alpine-Nordic combinations, cross-country skiing here shares the amenities of the well-established downhill facility. Yet, there is a rustic Touring Center that seems built around a huge wood stove and offers Nordic aficionados everything they will want or need. The intermediate trails are pretty and varied. Skiing begins on farm fields sectioned by ancient stone walls, then proceeds to brookside trails that run through cathedral-like stands of pine and birch forest. There is plenty of touring off the trail as well, leading experts up the flank of Mt. Cobble and into the notch between Cobble and Gunstock. From the high terrain you overlook Lake Winnipesaukee. From here, for the hearty, there is a 3-mile racing loop that skirts Cobble and returns to the hospitable base lodge.

LOON MOUNTAIN CROSS-COUNTRY CENTER
RR1, Box 41
Lincoln, New Hampshire 03251
(603) 745–8111, Extension 5568

HOURS: 8:00 A.M. to 5:00 P.M.

TRAIL SYSTEM: 35 kilometers (about 23 miles)

TRAIL DIFFICULTY: Easiest, more difficult, most difficult

TRAIL GROOMING: Daily; skate-groomed and trackset

RENTAL EQUIPMENT: Yes

INSTRUCTION: Yes; PSIA-certified

FOOD FACILITIES: Lunches available at the base lodge

LODGING: A forty-unit inn at the mountain, as well as several rental condominiums through the Loon reservation service

HOW TO GET THERE: I–93 to Exit 32; Route 112 east in New Hampshire, then Loon Mountain Road

Though touring at this popular Alpine area has all the advantages and drawbacks that go along with sharing facilities with downhill types, the Loon trails lead you quickly into the wilderness of the Pemigewasset National Forest. Skiing here follows a spider web of old logging roads and deer paths, with sudden views of the Franconia Range of the White Mountains. Trails course through the deep solitude of snow-impacted stream beds and slab up the sides of steep hills in spots. They are well marked. The trail system also employs the Alpine slopes for you to go out on your Telemark skinny skis and show the jellybeans what real skiing is. The nightlife at Loon holds countless opportunities for the tireless.

PERRY HOLLOW CROSS-COUNTRY CENTER
New Durham, New Hampshire 03894
(603) 569–3055

HOURS: 8:30 A.M. to 4:30 P.M.

TRAIL SYSTEM: 25 kilometers (about 15 miles)

TRAIL DIFFICULTY: Easiest, more difficult, most difficult

TRAIL GROOMING: All groomed; 15 kilometers trackset; 5 kilometers skating

RENTAL EQUIPMENT: Yes

INSTRUCTION: Ski school; group lessons

FOOD FACILITIES: Snacks available

LODGING: Inns and motels in the area

HOW TO GET THERE: From Route 95 at Portsmouth take Spaulding Turnpike to Rochester, then follow Route 11 to New Durham

Perry Hollow is a broad trail system that allows for all kinds of skiing, from the traditional tours in the woods to high-speed skating on a 5-kilometer track. The area is located in the easy-to-reach region of southern New Hampshire near the lower reaches of Winnipesaukee. When the snow is right, the skiing is excellent with room enough for all tastes.

WINDBLOWN CROSS-COUNTRY SKI CENTER

RFD 2, Box 669
New Ipswich, New Hampshire 03071
(603) 878–2869

HOURS: 9:00 A.M. to 5:00 P.M.

TRAIL SYSTEM: 40 kilometers (about 24 miles)

TRAIL DIFFICULTY: Easiest, more difficult, most difficult

TRAIL GROOMING: 15 kilometers groomed daily; skating lanes. Some night skiing

RENTAL EQUIPMENT: 125 sets

INSTRUCTION: Weekends; by appointment on weekdays

FOOD FACILITIES: Soup and sandwiches available

LODGING: Inns and motels in the area. Warming hut available overnight by arrangement; sleeps twelve

HOW TO GET THERE: Route 2 heading west to Leomenster, exit at Route 13 north, follow into Townsend; head west on Route 119. Turn right at sign for New Ipswich, Route 124. Facility is 11 miles up on left.

This high-elevation touring center in the sweeping Monadnock countryside usually has a long season, pushing well into April most years. It is a full-amenity center with a good base lodge complete with rentals, retail shop, waxing room, and a simple hearty kitchen for trail's end when skiers kick their feet up in front of the radiant wood stove. Deep in the middle of the 19-mile trail system there is a warming hut in the woods for ski-hikers to lay out a bedroll for the night or for day skiers to stop for lunch. There are three other shelters in the woods as well.

NORSK CROSS-COUNTRY SKI CENTER

Route 11, Box 735
New London, New Hampshire 03257
(603) 526–4685

HOURS: 9:00 A.M. to 5:00 P.M.

TRAIL SYSTEM: 90 kilometers (55 miles)

TRAIL DIFFICULTY: Easiest, more difficult, most difficult

TRAIL GROOMING: Groomed and trackset

RENTAL EQUIPMENT: 150 sets

INSTRUCTION: Classes at 10:30 A.M., noon, and 1:00 P.M., by arrangment

FOOD FACILITIES: Restaurant and lounge on premises

LODGING: Inn on the premises. Separate phone: (603) 526–6040

HOW TO GET THERE: I–93 to I–89 to Exit 11; east 1½ miles past Grey House Restaurant to the first right-hand turn

This touring center on the skirts of Mt. Kearsarge offers some excellent large and varied terrain for touring in the region. All trails are well groomed and well marked; the loops are intelligently conceived, both for novice skiers looking for their first short loop and for experts who want to run a marathon through these foothills. One of the nicest features is that Norsk is a major-sized area just two hours from Boston near Sunapee and King Ridge—two Alpine areas made for Nordic whizzes who are ready to try out their Telemark technique. Norsk has a full spate of services, including rentals, retail gear, food, and lodging at the nice, white-gabled Lake Sunapee Country Club and Inn. Excellent maps are available, as are special events—from moonlight tours to sauna tours to racing, skating, and Telemark workshops.

DEER CAP SKI TOURING CENTER

Route 16
Ossipee, New Hampshire 03814
(603) 539–6030

HOURS: 8:30 A.M. to 4:30 P.M.

TRAIL SYSTEM: 20 kilometers (about 13 miles)

TRAIL DIFFICULTY: Easiest, more difficult, most difficult

TRAIL GROOMING: Groomed and trackset as needed

RENTAL EQUIPMENT: 100 sets

INSTRUCTION: By appointment only

FOOD FACILITIES: Trail snacks at the center

LODGING: Inns and motels in the area within 2 miles

HOW TO GET THERE: I-95 to Portsmouth, New Hampshire; Spaulding Turnpike to Route 16 north to Center Ossipee

Think you're a hotshot? Think you can bring a little place like Deer Cap to its knees with your dazzle? Then the Superstar trail is for you. Deer Cap may not have much expert terrain, but this windy, snaggy heart-stopper will be taken seriously by skiers on every level since it is one of the toughest you can find. Most of the trails here wind through pretty, fairly flat terrain in pine woods. The lodge has an eating center with a snack bar, rest rooms, and plenty of room to wax your skis. The trails begin just outside the door.

TEMPLE MOUNTAIN CROSS-COUNTRY SKI AREA

Route 101, Box 368
Peterborough, New Hampshire 03458
(603) 924–6949

HOURS: 9:00 A.M. to 4:30 P.M.

TRAIL SYSTEM: 43 kilometers (about 26 miles)

TRAIL DIFFICULTY: Easiest, more difficult, most difficult

TRAIL GROOMING: 8 kilometers groomed, 6 of them trackset. Some skating lanes

RENTAL EQUIPMENT: More than 100 sets

INSTRUCTION: Yes, both weekdays and weekends. Check the schedule

FOOD FACILITIES: Cafeteria and lounge in the main lodge

LODGING: None on the mountain; several hotels, motels, and inns in the region

HOW TO GET THERE: Route 3 north to Nashua; Route 101A to 101 West to Peterborough to Temple Mountain

Several improvements have changed this already excellent and well-appointed ski-touring area. Many of the trails have been widened and improved, with new terrain being opened all the time. More and more of the terrain is being tracked, and a new Telemark program has been designed, making use of the broad downhill trails on Temple.

At an elevation between 1,500 and 2,000 feet, Temple usually records an annual snowfall of between 10 and 14 feet and is a paradise for powderhounds no matter what they have on their feet. Add to this much snow the fact that Temple is less than 70 miles from Boston, and you have the makings of a major ski-touring area for the snow-starved folks from New England's flatlands.

The skiing, which combines its own large system with the 20-mile Wapack Trail, takes tourers across fir-ringed mountain ridges with sudden dramatic overlooks; then the trail may plunge down across meadowland into hardwood groves and stream beds. For the adventurous, narrower trails wind off the beaten path through thickets of snow-heavy evergreen boughs and lead skiers into day-long wilderness tours. There are several shelters scattered throughout the trail system. The area also provides a full variety of skier services. Cafeteria-style food is available in the lodge.

SNOWVILLAGE INN

Snowville, New Hampshire 03849
(603) 447–2818

HOURS: 9:00 A.M. to 9:00 P.M. For guests only

TRAIL SYSTEM: 13 kilometers (about 8 miles); downhill ski trails also available nearby

TRAIL DIFFICULTY: Easiest, more difficult, most difficult

TRAIL GROOMING: Some; limited skating

RENTAL EQUIPMENT: Yes

INSTRUCTION: Weekends, or weekdays by appointment

FOOD FACILITIES: Full meals and bar available at Snowvillage Inn

LODGING: Snowvillage Inn, plus inns and motels throughout the Mount Washington Valley

HOW TO GET THERE: I–95 to Spaulding Turnpike to Route 16 heading north to Conway; Route 153 to sign for Snowville and Brownfield; at Snowville, right on Foss Mountain Road

With good reason, the Snowvillage Inn, an Edwardian estate in the lap of Mt. Washington, 1,100 feet high in its foothills, has gained the reputation as one of the most spectacular winter vacation spots in the region. Though only 6 miles out of Conway, the inn is secluded in the upper woodlands of Foss Mountain; from the porch guests have a sweeping panoramic view of the valley, with Mt. Washington itself looming over the place, close enough to touch, it seems.

The skiing is of the woodland variety with groomed and track-set trails (150 acres) that take skiers into thickets and out again for sudden high-altitude overviews of the valley. The skiing is lovely, convenient, and thoroughly accommodated to tourers. But it is the inn that cuts Snowvillage above the ordinary. With its 19 cozy bedrooms, and the crackling fire in a big country living room cluttered with books, magazines, and dozing dogs, this inn is as honestly homey and convivial as they come. In the dining room guests are served multicourse gourmet meals, beginning, perhaps, with Hungarian mushroom soup and ending with Cognac back at the fire. It is difficult to exaggerate the elegance and charm of the Snowvillage Inn in its après-ski mode.

SUNSET HILL TOURING CENTER

Sugar Hill, New Hampshire 03585
(603) 823–5522

HOURS: 8:00 A.M. to dusk

TRAIL SYSTEM: 60 kilometers (about 40 miles)

TRAIL DIFFICULTY: Easiest, more difficult, most difficult

TRAIL GROOMING: 15 kilometers groomed daily; some skating

RENTAL EQUIPMENT: 100 sets

INSTRUCTION: Yes

FOOD FACILITIES: Soup is served at the touring center; full meals at the inn

LODGING: Thirty-five rooms at the inn

HOW TO GET THERE: I–93 to Franconia; Route 117 traveling west to Sunset Hill

Atop Sugar Hill in the White Mountains sits the Sunset House, an old New England inn with nice flavor of its own and excellent, nearly limitless skiing possibilities. Its own trails run into the Franconia Inn network, as well as a few other trail systems in this well-toured region. Skiers can slide all day over the lower flats of the valley or chug up through the timber-ringed upper plateaus for an overview of the impressive geography of the region. Back at the Sunset Hill Center, skiers like to hang out at the ski shop with its kettle of homemade soup simmering on the stove. All the amenities are available, from instruction to rental and retail equipment. This is also the place to sign up for guided day and moonlight tours. The inn has a fine restaurant for food and drink; it offers high-quality lodging.

THE INN AT EAST HILL FARM
460 Monadnock Street
Troy, New Hampshire 03465
(603) 242–6495

HOURS: Daylight

TRAIL SYSTEM: 14 kilometers (about 9 miles)

TRAIL DIFFICULTY: Easiest, more difficult, most difficult

TRAIL GROOMING: As needed. Trackset

RENTAL EQUIPMENT: 130 sets

INSTRUCTION: Yes

FOOD FACILITIES: Full restaurant at the inn, serving breakfast, lunch, and dinner

LODGING: Cottages available; rooms at the inn

HOW TO GET THERE: I–91 to Brattleboro, Vermont; Route 9 east to Keene, New Hampshire; Route 12 south to Troy; left on Jaffrey Road to the inn

East Hill Farm is one of those country inns that, while not monumental in size and scope, does many things with excellence. Most notably, all the terrain here is gentle and appealing, with its lovely scenery around the base of Mt. Monadnock. The farm itself is also appealing, producing delicious country-style meals and offering indoor swimming, sauna, and a skating rink. East Hill Farm is a complete and well-appointed touring destination.

WATERVILLE VALLEY CROSS-COUNTRY SKI AREA

Box 247
Waterville Valley, New Hampshire 03215
(603) 236–4666

HOURS: 9:00 A.M. to 4:30 P.M., all week
TRAIL SYSTEM: 105 kilometers (about 63 miles)
TRAIL DIFFICULTY: Easiest, more difficult, most difficult
TRAIL GROOMING: Yes; both traditional trackset and skating lanes
RENTAL EQUIPMENT: Yes
INSTRUCTION: PSIA-certified
FOOD FACILITIES: Finish Line Restaurant at the Touring Center
LODGING: Several inns and rental condominiums
HOW TO GET THERE: I–93 north to Exit 28; Route 49 east to Waterville Valley

Waterville Valley is one of the major Alpine ski centers in the Northeast and in recent years has become a self-contained ski village for all sizes, styles, and levels of the sport. Using all the meadows and woods in the region, cross-country buffs have nearly unlimited touring. On the more organized trail system, skiers will follow miles of old logging roads, starting from a cluster of rustic buildings that comprise the center. The trail web rolls outward from this spot, a carefully graded, marked, and groomed system. Some trails roll through gentle woodland flats, while others mount precipitously toward high-country plateaus and nice vistas of the surrounding mountains. Alpine and Nordic forms mix at Waterville when it is time for coaches at the school to give Telemark instruction. The teaching also features demonstrations, workshops of all kinds, and video teaching. For an extra charge, skiers can access the Snow's Mountain trails via the double chairlift and descend the gently pitched downhill trails on Snow Mountain. Look for a full complement of rental and retail goods, and ask about the race program. This is a world-class ski area with many top-shelf events in its list of credits. For those who like nightlife and/or elegant dining, there are some good bars and restaurants in the village. Most skiing and social life is centered around the new Town Square village center.

THE NORDIC SKIER

47 North Main Street
Wolfeboro, New Hampshire 03894
(603) 569–3151

HOURS: 9:00 A.M. to 5:30 P.M.

TRAIL SYSTEM: 20 kilometers (about 12 miles)

TRAIL DIFFICULTY: Easiest, more difficult, most difficult

TRAIL GROOMING: Yes; trackset with 7 kilometers of skating lanes

RENTAL EQUIPMENT: 100 sets

INSTRUCTION: PSIA-certified

FOOD FACILITIES: In the town and area

LODGING: In the town and area

HOW TO GET THERE: I–93N to Exit Route 3; north to Route 28 North to Wolfeboro

Wolfeboro is a fishing town. Summer and winter, the folks talk fishing, anticipate it, clean up after it, and get ready for more. Yet there is a certain season after the first snow falls in November, when another kind of sportsman comes into Wolfeboro—the touring skier. Along with snowmobilers and ice fishermen, the town also becomes the cross-country center of the Lakes Region. There are two newly designed separate trail systems that offer a variety of experiences (though without the real toe-curling black terrain)—the more challenging Abenaki Trails, and the Lakeview network for novice or easy skiing. There are also plenty of woods, unplowed logging roads, and wilderness skiing for off-track aficionados. There is a good touring specialty shop at hand in Wolfeboro as the town has come to cater to skiers. Rentals, guides, retail gear, instruction, and all sorts of moonlight skiing and workshops are available here as well. Good food and lodging abound in wide variety.

MAINE

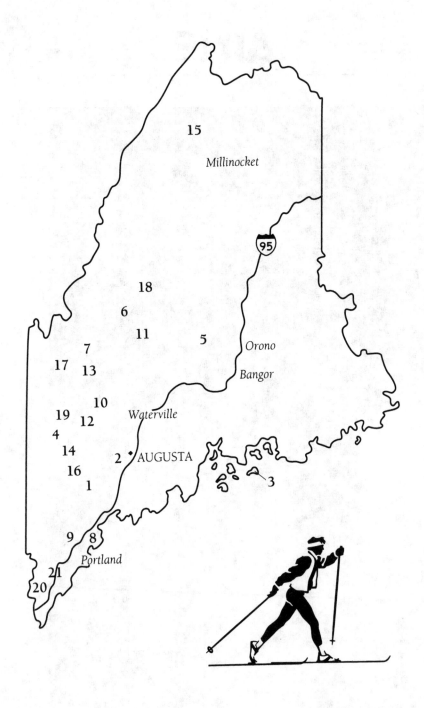

15

Millinocket

I-95

18

6

11

5

Orono

Bangor

7

17

13

10

Waterville

19

12

4

14

2 • AUGUSTA

16

1

3

9 8

Portland

21

20

MAINE

Numbers on map refer to towns numbered below

SNORADA RECREATION CENTER

525 Lake Street
Auburn, Maine 04210
(207) 748–0191

HOURS: Monday through Friday, 11:00 A.M. to 9:00 P.M.; weekends, 9:00 A.M. to 9:00 P.M. (Night skiing on a lighted trail loop)

TRAIL SYSTEM: 15 kilometers (about 10 miles); groomed, trackset, skating lanes. Some wilderness

TRAIL DIFFICULTY: Easiest, more difficult, most difficult

TRAIL GROOMING: Groomed and trackset

RENTAL EQUIPMENT: Yes

INSTRUCTION: Lessons by appointment

FOOD FACILITIES: Snack bar at center; full restaurants within ½ mile of the center

LODGING: In Auburn

HOW TO GET THERE: Maine Turnpike to Exit 12 in Auburn; after tolls take a left on Washington Avenue and follow downtown through three sets of lights. Left on Court Street and bear right onto Lake Street; the center is about 2 miles up Lake Street.

This cosmopolitan touring center is the site of the Bates College Winter Carnival and plenty of citizen racing, including a Bill Koch League and Tuesday-night races that give it a rather vigorous cast. The terrain varies from open field to some woods running loops, over two somewhat challenging ridges and across a frozen lake. It is fine touring, and there are plans to expand the trail system. The center has rental and retail equipment and provides a waxing room and trail snacks.

NATANIS CROSS-COUNTRY SKI TRAILS

RFD 1, Box 554
Augusta, Maine 04330
(207) 622–6533

HOURS: December 26 to March 1, Monday to Friday, 9:00 A.M. to dark; weekends, dawn to dusk

TRAIL SYSTEM: 10 kilometers (about 6 miles)

TRAIL DIFFICULTY: Easiest, more difficult

TRAIL GROOMING: Trackset, skating

RENTAL EQUIPMENT: Yes

INSTRUCTION: For beginners

FOOD FACILITIES: Trail snacks available at the center; full restaurant meals within 4 miles

LODGING: Motel within 4 miles

HOW TO GET THERE: Maine Turnpike to Augusta, then Route 201 traveling north. After passing Cony High School in Augusta, the center is 8 miles on Route 201

Beginning with open field warm-ups, the Natanis trails take skiers through deep forest where, despite the proximity to the city, an abundance of wildlife makes its presence known. You'll see signs of moose, deer, rabbit, and fox as you ski over this rolling terrain. One trail leads out to a beaver bog, where the animals have felled trees to build their lodges to hibernate the winter away. Not a heavy challenge for the mountain-man skier, Natanis is nevertheless a pretty, well-run ski area. Town-sponsored citizen races and moonlight tours are part of the fun here.

ACADIA NATIONAL PARK
Box 177
Bar Harbor, Maine 04609
(207) 288–3338

HOURS: 24 hours a day; headquarters, 8:30 A.M. to 4:30 P.M.

TRAIL SYSTEM: 79 kilometers (about 49 miles) for ski touring and snowshoeing only

TRAIL DIFFICULTY: Easiest, more difficult

TRAIL GROOMING: None

RENTAL EQUIPMENT: Ski shops in the area

INSTRUCTION: None

FOOD FACILITIES: Nearby

LODGING: Nearby

HOW TO GET THERE: Maine Turnpike to Route 3, follow through Ellsworth to Bar Harbor; right on Route 233 for 3 miles to park headquarters

Acadia National Park is one of the splendid natural wonders of New England and a longstanding attraction for millions of summertime visitors. In winter, however, this coastal forest with its glimpses of the stormy, rock-bound coast and the steady sea roar is quite a moving experience for most skiers. Nature can overwhelm you here just a bit, and you return, even from a three-hour trip, feeling you have been far away for a long time. The park authority has done a good job separating the ski-trail system from snowmobiles—and giving skiers nearly 50 miles to themselves. The trail loops are built over the wide, gravel-packed carriage roads. Though ungroomed, most are trackset by previous skiers.

There are loops of just an hour or two, or routes that incorporate a day's skiing through the snow-laden woods, over ice-crusted, gurgling brooks, and into places like Eagle Lake and Jordan Pond. One route takes skiers nearly across to Somes Sound and Northeast Harbor at the seaward end of the pennisula—Maine's Motif Number One. For day skiers who pack a trail lunch and take off, good trail maps are available at the ranger station. Toilet facilities are available near Eagle Lake.

BETHEL INN CROSS-COUNTRY SKI CENTER

P.O. Box 49
Bethel, Maine 04217
(207) 824–2175

HOURS: 8:00 A.M. to 5:00 P.M.

TRAIL SYSTEM: 40 kilometers (about 24 miles)

TRAIL DIFFICULTY: Easiest, more difficult, most difficult

TRAIL GROOMING: Yes, on all terrain; skating on 15 kilometers

RENTAL EQUIPMENT: Yes

INSTRUCTION: Group and private lessons daily, including Telemarking

FOOD FACILITIES: Main dining room or library open for breakfast and dinner; soups and sandwiches available in the tavern at lunchtime

LODGING: At the inn

HOW TO GET THERE: Maine Turnpike to Exit 11; Route 26 north into Bethel

The Bethel Inn hardly needs an introduction to aficionados of the rural Northeast. It is a New England classic, its stately colonial yellow dominating the twin-spired Bethel Common. The entire area is a National Historic District. In summer the inn is a plush country club, in winter a first-rate ski-touring center nestled in the foothills of the White Mountains. Skiers begin right out the back door of the inn, warm up on the golf course, then plunge into the wide, well-marked wooded trails that cross frozen streams and then open into sudden panoramic views of the Longfellow Range. Most trails are made up of gently curving, undulating terrain, just right for beginners and intermediates. However, experts are invited to try their Telemarking technique on Corkscrew or the Peter Grover Hill. The latter is especially steep and good for Telemark—or Alpine—skiing.

At breakfast, skiers may purchase box lunches for the trail. Our favorite picnic tour is out to the Lake House, where skiers relax and eat in front of the big fieldstone fireplace. Après-ski is casual and friendly—piano-bar entertainment on weekends with drinks, sauna, and board games of all kinds. The inn also offers evening sleigh rides.

CARTER'S CROSS-COUNTRY SKI CENTER

Route 28
Bethel, Maine 04270
(207) 539–4848

HOURS: 9:00 A.M. to dark

TRAIL SYSTEM: 65 kilometers (about 38 miles)

TRAIL DIFFICULTY: Easiest, more difficult, most difficult

TRAIL GROOMING: Groomed and trackset when possible; skating trails available

RENTAL EQUIPMENT: Yes

INSTRUCTION: Yes

FOOD FACILITIES: Snacks and beverages available at the site

LODGING: Two lodge facilities with rental cabins; a Mongolian yurt is used as a warming hut, and may be rented nightly

HOW TO GET THERE: Follow Route 95 to the Maine Turnpike. Turn off at Exit 11 and follow Route 26 going north past Oxford to Bethel

With the low-snow winters of late, Dave and Ann Carter, owners of the other Carter area in Oxford, located a second touring center in the higher country of Bethel. When there's little to no cover just 30 miles down at Oxford, the Bethel site gets plenty of natural cover. Aside from the huge, varied trail system, the Mountain Trail leads 2½ miles up the mountain, opening spectacular views of the Androscoggin River Valley and the Presidential Range. As much fun as it is to ski up the mountain, skiing back down is a rush. There's plenty of skiing here to challenge the experts, and beginners can also find lots of level ground to get their confidence in place before taking to the woods. The area has two lodging houses with ski-in cabins high up in the mountains.

SUNDAY RIVER CROSS-COUNTRY SKI CENTER

RFD 2, Box 1688
Bethel, Maine 04217
(207) 824–2410

HOURS: 9:00 A.M. to 5:00 P.M.

TRAIL SYSTEM: 40 kilometers (25 miles)

TRAIL DIFFICULTY: Easiest, more difficult, most difficult

TRAIL GROOMING: 25 kilometers groomed and trackset; 20 kilometers of skating lanes; 10 kilometers for experts

RENTAL EQUIPMENT: Yes

INSTRUCTION: Yes

FOOD FACILITIES: Trail snacks in the cross-country center; restaurant and lounge within ½ mile; access via road or ski trail

LODGING: Rooms available at Sunday River Inn; sleeping bag and dormitory living also available

HOW TO GET THERE: Maine Turnpike to Exit 11 at Gray; Route 26 to Bethel, then Routes 2, 5, and 26 through Bethel to the ski-area access road; signs to the center

Located in the beautifully wild Sunday River Valley, this cross-county center offers trails for all abilities and levels of enthusiasm. Beginners enjoy the level terrain in the pine woods near the center and soon accept the challenge of the 5-mile round trip along the valley floor to Artists' Covered Bridge. Intermediate and expert skiers appreciate the double trackset trails and have plenty of challenge with the longer, steeper trails that meander up and down the rolling hills through mixed forest growth to the trailside lean-to, the scenic overlook, and the fabled plunge known as David's Drop. The center offers night skiing by kerosene lamp on Fridays, special events throughout the winter, including the annual Sunday River 30-kilometer tour/race, and the popular season-transition triathlon, the April Fools' Day Pole, Paddle, and Paw Race, in late March. Sunday River is another of those Nordic centers that can take advantage of a well-developed Alpine area. Ths staff has also instituted a disabled skier training program.

LITTLE LYFORD POND LODGE

Box 688
Brownville, Maine 04414
(207) 695–2821 (via radio contact)

HOURS: Dawn to dusk
TRAIL SYSTEM: About 80 kilometers (50 miles)
TRAIL DIFFICULTY: Easiest, more difficult, most difficult
TRAIL GROOMING: Tracked but not groomed
RENTAL EQUIPMENT: None
INSTRUCTION: Informal
FOOD FACILITIES: Dining in the main lodge
LODGING: Insulated cabins with wood stoves
HOW TO GET THERE: Fly-in service from Greenville, Maine

Little Lyford is a backcountry destination area for a maximum of ten skiers. For the hearty, rather than flying in, you can ski in over a 10-kilometer trail. Daily touring is in the deep back woods of Maine's north country, over old logging roads and hardwood trails, along frozen stream beds, and over hidden ponds. Skiers will visit the spectacular Gulf Hagas Gorge and break the powder on the surrounding hillsides. The trail network varies from shorter, flatter routes to a challenging trek to the top of Elephant Mountain, or a 13-mile round-trip ski into Greenville. Also available by arrangement are custom inn-to-inn treks. After the daily touring, a sauna awaits tired bodies, and serious country dinners are served at the main lodge. Platform tennis is also available for the tireless.

STERLING INN
Route 201
Caratunk, Maine 04925
(800) 766–7238

HOURS: Daylight
TRAIL SYSTEM: Wilderness trails
TRAIL DIFFICULTY: Gentle to variable
TRAIL GROOMING: Some tracking with snowmobiles
RENTAL EQUIPMENT: Yes
INSTRUCTION: Guides, by appointment
FOOD FACILITIES: Yes, meals at the inn
LODGING: Yes, bed and breakfast rooms, plus cabins
HOW TO GET THERE: Follow Route 95 to Exit 36, then follow Route
201 heading north to Caratunk

This area is a white-water rafting center in the warm season, and when the lakes are frozen and Mount Katahdin is covered with snow, the skiing and snowshoeing among the moose is one of the great outdoor getaways. This region of Maine is accessible via the well-maintained roads and so is not the end of the Earth as it may look on a map of New England.

If you want skiing to yourself, here in the rolling hills that overlook the Kennebec River Valley near The Forks, you can ski hour after hour, breaking new trail or skiing over snowmobile-cleared track; without seeing another skier in your space.

Back at the inn, there are other winter activities, and they all involve the stunning wilderness surroundings. The West Forks, where the Dead and Kennebec rivers meet, is one of the natural wonders of the New England countryside. Ice fishing on Millinocket Lake, and taking home your landlocked salmon for the grill that night is a special treat. And of course, some ice-fishermen make use of their waiting time to take some skiing loops on the lake.

SUGARLOAF CROSS-COUNTRY SKI CENTER
Box 518
Carrabassett Valley, Maine 04947
(207) 237–2205

HOURS: 8:45 A.M. to 4:30 P.M.

TRAIL SYSTEM: 85 kilometers (about 51 miles); 5 kilometers of skating lanes; 12-kilometer racing track

TRAIL DIFFICULTY: Least difficult, more difficult, most difficult

TRAIL GROOMING: Most trails groomed as necessary. Some wilderness skiing along the Appalachian Trail

RENTAL EQUIPMENT: Yes

INSTRUCTION: PSIA-certifed

FOOD FACILITIES: Food served weekends and holidays

LODGING: Inns and motels in area. Call (207) 235–2100

HOW TO GET THERE: Maine Turnpike to Exit 12 at Auburn; Route 4 to Farmington, then Route 27 toward Kingfield. The touring center is a left turn 14 miles north of Kingfield, 1 mile from Sugarloaf Mountain, an Alpine area

This touring area is a groomed piece of New England's Big North Woods, and the place doesn't lose that wild feeling. Indeed, some of the excursions off the Appalachian Trail take skiers through the cedar bogs frequented by some of some of the region's large moose population. At the organized extreme, the area also takes its racing most seriously.

For novice skiers there are the wide, gently graded trails that run along the old narrow-gauge railroad bed; one favorite trail runs down along the Carrabassett River nearly to the door of the famous Red Stallion Inn. For more advanced skiers, the area has a well-marked trail system of steep verticals and descents through bogs and stream beds. The Touring Center sells good maps, provides rentals and lessons, and offers all the amenities, from hot homemade food to waxing clinics and moonlight excursions. A skating rink is also available. There is plenty of lodging available through the Sugarloaf Reservation Service at (207) 237–2861.

VAL HALLA COUNTRY CLUB AND CROSS-COUNTRY SKI CENTER

Val Halla Road
Cumberland, Maine 04021
(207) 829–3700

HOURS: 9:00 A.M. to 4:00 P.M.

TRAIL SYSTEM: 25 kilometers (about 16 miles)

TRAIL DIFFICULTY: Easiest, more difficult, most difficult

TRAIL GROOMING: Yes

RENTAL EQUIPMENT: Yes

INSTRUCTION: No

FOOD FACILITIES: Snack bar and lounge at the Country Club; full restaurants within 15 miles

LODGING: Hotels and motels within 10 miles

HOW TO GET THERE: Maine Turnpike to Exit 9; Route 1, Tuttle Road, Middle Road, then Greely Road to Val Halla Road

This touring center is a good example of the growing popularity of country-club ski touring. An already established golf facility turns nicely into a ski center with all the amenities and very nice terrain for cross-country runs and tours. Val Halla is in the Casco Bay region of the state, near both Portland and Freeport, the now-famous home of L. L. Bean. The skiing itself is gentle on the open flats, then rolling in the surrounding woods with streams and ponds. In places the rolling terrain rolls into quite a challenge for skiers of any level.

HARRIS FARM STAND SKI TOURING

Buzzel Road
Dayton, Maine 04005
(207) 499–2678

HOURS: 8:30 A.M. to dusk

TRAIL SYSTEM: More than 30 kilometers (18 miles) of trails and open field skiing

TRAIL DIFFICULTY: Easiest, more difficult, most difficult

TRAIL GROOMING: Trails are groomed and trackset
RENTAL EQUIPMENT: Yes
INSTRUCTION: Yes
FOOD FACILITIES: Snacks available in the warming shed
LODGING: Inns in the region
HOW TO GET THERE: Take the Maine Turnpike to Kennebunk Exit, then follow Route 35 north. Turn right onto Gould Road, then right on Buzzell Road. Ski area will be on the right.

Harris Farm covers 500 acres of lovely rolling farmland and woods and offers a variety of open and sheltered skiing. Trails range from gentle beginner loops to steep rolling hills for advanced skiers. The forest is part of the American Tree Farm system and offers plenty of trail variety, from flatter wide trails to chutes and upland treks. Trails are nicely groomed throughout the winter. The area is near enough the tourist town of Kennebunkport to offer an excellent variety of lodging, dining, and shopping opportunities après-ski.

TITCOMB MOUNTAIN SKI TOURING CENTER
Morrison Hill Road
Farmington, Maine 04938
(207) 778–9031

HOURS: Tuesday through Friday, 1:00 to 4:00 P.M.; Saturday and Sunday, 9:00 A.M. to 4:00 P.M.

TRAIL SYSTEM: 25 kilometers (about 15 miles); unlimited wilderness

TRAIL DIFFICULTY: Easiest, more difficult, most difficult

TRAIL GROOMING: Yes

RENTAL EQUIPMENT: Nearby in Farmington

INSTRUCTION: Yes

FOOD FACILITIES: Lunch available at the lodge; several restaurants nearby

LODGING: Several inns and motels in the area

HOW TO GET THERE: Maine Turnpike to the Auburn, Maine, exit; Route 4 north to Farmington

In the foothills of the Longfellow Mountains in west-central Maine, the Titcomb trails—mostly beginner and intermediate—roll over gentle hills and through meadows and fir forest. The trail system accesses an additional 15 miles of trails in the woods, one of them leading to a downtown restaurant in this pretty college-campus town. Through the Farmington Ski Club, Titcomb offers citizen racing, ski jumping, and Telemark practice on the nearby Alpine area. The large lodge has a lunch counter, rest rooms, and changing and waxing rooms. Lessons are given each afternoon, by appointment.

TROLL VALLEY CROSS-COUNTRY CENTER

Red Schoolhouse Road
Farmington, Maine 04938
(207) 778–3656

HOURS: 9:00 A.M. to dusk

TRAIL SYSTEM: 30 kilometers (about 18 miles)

TRAIL DIFFICULTY: Easiest, more difficult, most difficult

TRAIL GROOMING: All trails groomed and trackset

RENTAL EQUIPMENT: Yes

INSTRUCTION: Yes

FOOD FACILITIES: Lunch counter and dining room

LODGING: Inns in the area

HOW TO GET THERE: Get off Route 95 at Auburn, and follow Route 4 to Farmington. Between Wilton and Farmington Centers, Red Schoolhouse Roads runs off Route 4 to the left

Established in 1985 as a cross-country and fitness center, Troll Valley is in the snowbelt of Western Maine, keeping it operating on an average of 105 days per winter. The trail network is laid out over about 300 acres of what was once rolling farmland. Replacing the old farmhouse is a modern lodge with food and equipment service, replete with a crackling fire. The trails vary from open-field skiing to beaver bogs and cedar swamps. The rolling hillsides offer some very challenging up- and downhill treks, and all trails are wide enough (12 to 20 feet) for a track along the sides with skating in the middle of the trail.

Off-trail skiing is nearly limitless at this area, and the adventurous skier finds himself in the foothills of the Longfellow Mountains with spectacular views of these hills and the flatlands of the Sandy River Plantation.

CRAB APPLE INN
The Forks, Maine 04985
(207) 663–2218

HOURS: No set hours

TRAIL SYSTEM: About 95 kilometers (about 55 miles); access to unlimited wilderness

TRAIL DIFFICULTY: Easiest, more difficult, most difficult

TRAIL GROOMING: None, except by snowmobiles that use the area

RENTAL EQUIPMENT: None

INSTRUCTION: No

FOOD FACILITIES: Breakfast and dinner by reservation at the inn; lunch snacks at the nearby general store

LODGING: Seven rooms at the inn; housekeeping cottage

HOW TO GET THERE: Maine Turnpike to Exit 36; Route 201 for 62 miles to The Forks

Overlooking a dramatic sweep of the Kennebec River, Crab Apple Inn offers seven rooms as well as a guest house with housekeeping privileges. This is North Country skiing in the true sense of that term, as the old logging roads here criss-cross infinitely, it seems, through deep wilderness forest, along the river valley, and up over mountain ridges along the trail along which Benedict Arnold marched his troops to Quebec. That wonderful city, incidentally, is just 140 miles from the inn.

Everyone at some point should have the experience of skiing into Moxie Falls—the highest waterfall in New England—or explore The Forks itself, a point of land at the confluence of the Dead and Kennebec rivers. Available from the inn are guided backcountry tours where trekkers cannot help but run across signs of snowshoe hare, deer, and moose. This is not for experts only, by the way, as the riverside trails along the Kennebec are gentle and groomed out by snowmobiles. This is true New England wilderness skiing several light years from civilization. In summer, it is a marvelous whitewater rafting center.

SPRUCE MOUNTAIN CROSS-COUNTRY CENTER

RFD 2, Box 8425
Jay, Maine 04239
(207) 897–0490

HOURS: Dawn to dusk, December to April

TRAIL SYSTEM: 15 kilometers (about 9 miles)

TRAIL DIFFICULTY: Easiest, more difficult, most difficult

TRAIL GROOMING: Groomed and trackset; skating lanes

RENTAL EQUIPMENT: No

INSTRUCTION: No

FOOD FACILITIES: At the Alpine hill

LODGING: In the Farmington area or Lewiston area, within 10 to 18 miles

HOW TO GET THERE: Maine Turnpike to Exit 12; Route 4 north, turn right before the bridge into Livermore Falls. The center is 1/2 mile down the river.

Spruce Mountain is a small area run in conjunction with the Spruce Mountain Alpine area on the west bank of the Androscoggin River. When the Alpine slopes are in operation, a snack bar is available. The trails vary in length and difficulty, from rolling riverside roadways to some challenging up-and-down loops that provide Alpine trails for Telemarking.

WINTER'S INN SKI TOURING CENTER

Box 44
Kingfield, Maine 04947
(207) 265–5421

HOURS: 9:00 A.M. to dusk

TRAIL SYSTEM: 30 kilometers (about 19 miles)

TRAIL DIFFICULTY: Easiest, more difficult

TRAIL GROOMING: No

RENTAL EQUIPMENT: Yes

INSTRUCTION: No

FOOD FACILITIES: Breakfast and dinner at the inn; lunches within skiing distance of the center

LODGING: Winter's Inn has twelve rooms; several motels and inns in the area

HOW TO GET THERE: Maine Turnpike to the second Augusta exit; Route 27 north to Kingfield

Here, in one of the most dramatic mountain areas in the Northeast—the Bigelow Range overlooking the Carrabassett Valley—Winter's Inn sits on a small hilltop overlooking the village of Kingfield. This restored Victorian country mansion was originally designed by the Stanley Brothers who invented the Stanley Steamer. It has five working fireplaces, a genial atmosphere, and plenty of art objects and antiques to look at. The inn overlooks Bigelow, Mt. Abrams, and Mt. Blue, as well as one of New England's true classic Alpine areas, Sugarloaf/USA.

Skiers have nearly limitless terrain at their disposal on wilderness trails carved from old logging roads, down through pine glades to the West Branch of the Carrabassett River. Here the wildlife is abundant, the skiing varied and vigorous. There is also open-field skiing through gently rolling uplands. For Telemark aficionados, Sugarloaf has plenty of terrain both gentle and steep. This big-country region can be skied season after season without giving up all her secrets and surprises to skiers.

MOUNT ABRAM SKI TOURING
Box 193
Locke Mills, Maine 04255
(207) 875–5003

HOURS: 9:00 A.M. to 4:00 P.M.

TRAIL SYSTEM: 14 kilometers (about 9 miles)

TRAIL DIFFICULTY: Easiest, more difficult, most difficult

TRAIL GROOMING: Groomed and trackset; no skating

RENTAL EQUIPMENT: Yes

INSTRUCTION: By appointment

FOOD FACILITIES: Cafeteria for lunches in the lodge

LODGING: In Bethel or West Paris, about 10 miles away

HOW TO GET THERE: Maine Turnpike to Exit 11, then Route 26 to Locke Mills

Mount Abram Ski Touring center is nestled beside Alpine slopes, allowing skiers to make use of Telemark terrain, as well as the skier facilities already there. After skiing along the base of the downhill slopes, tourers plunge into the snow-laden hardwood and pine trails, following old logging roads, stream beds, and small bridges crisscrossing Putt Brook. This is picturesque terrain, easy to negotiate, though there are some challenging climbs, twists, turns, and descents on some of the trails. Moonlight tours are available along a wide trail, and citizen races are encouraged here, including the annual Bob Cole Cup Race.

BAXTER STATE PARK

64 Balsam Drive
Millinocket, Maine 04462
(207) 723-5839

HOURS: Daylight, December through March

TRAIL SYSTEM: Wilderness trails in a 100-square-mile tract

TRAIL DIFFICULTY: Easiest, more difficult, most difficult

TRAIL GROOMING: None

RENTAL EQUIPMENT: No

INSTRUCTION: No

FOOD FACILITIES: In Millinocket, about 25 miles away

LODGING: In Millinocket

HOW TO GET THERE: I-95 to Millinocket, then Greenville Road to the Baxter State Park entrance 18 miles past town

Though Baxter State Park is on a well-worn path of Maine's summertime delights, in winter, it is a remote wild land of fierce weather and tough outdoor challenges. Thus, touring here should be considered only by the most experienced woodsman-skier who has a working knowledge of what winter means in this deep northern country (though the skiing itself need not be the hairest, espe-

cially with the miles of flattish logging roads between Millinocket and Greenville). Winter camping is available in a limited number of bunkhouses, lean-tos, tents, and igloos. Skiers must either bush-whack in to the Park Headquarters, or take the Golden Road, sharing it with lumber carriers bringing pulp wood to the mill.

All the caveats aside, however, this is wonderful backwoods country along one of the most spectacular watercourses in the Northeast—the West Branch of the Penobscot River. The snow-covered bulk of Mt. Katahdin looms over the land (it may not be climbed in winter, incidentally). For skiers who truly want to break away from the crowds, and who are confident of their outdoor skills, Baxter State Park is among the finest wilderness ski expeditions to be found anywhere.

KATAHDIN LAKE WILDERNESS CAMPS

Box 389
Millinocket, Maine 04462

HOURS: Daily, dawn to dusk
TRAIL SYSTEM: 48 kilometers (30 miles)
TRAIL DIFFICULTY: More difficult, most difficult wilderness trails
TRAIL GROOMING: No
RENTAL EQUIPMENT: No
INSTRUCTION: No
FOOD FACILITIES: Yes
LODGING: At the camp center and camps
HOW TO GET THERE: I–95 to Route 157 to Millinocket Lake. Here, either fly-in or ski-in access; there is no auto road.

On the remote shores of Katahdin Lake, these wilderness camps are the gateway to real outback trekking experience. Like many such guided tours, skiing skill and experience are not the critical factors. Rather, Katahdin's tours are for adventurous folks in fairly good physical shape who are flexible enough to trade amenities for stunning wilderness adventure. Being in decent shape, though, is a starter.

The tour begins with a fly-in (or ski-in) to the camps along the frozen shore of the beautiful Katahdin Lake, about 30 miles north of Millinocket. If you ski from the lake, where you'll leave your car, to the camps, it is a full-day, 20-mile trek. However, Scotty's Flying Service at Shin Pond will be happy to take you in. It takes about twelve minutes by plane.

At the camp center there are American Plan accommodations with family-style meals. Aside from this there are no rental or retail goods available, so skiers must bring what is necessary for a few days of trekking—from clothes and equipment to waxes. One tip: Bring a camera. You'll be touring in some of the most astounding backcountry anywhere, a place where "the only nightlife you will hear will be a distant owl or coyote in the hills," in the words of director Al Cooper. In the morning the tracks of a grouse, moose, or pine marten crossing your trail may tell you that you are not completely alone in this beautiful winter world.

ROBINSON TWIN PINE CAMPS

P.O. Box 152
Millinocket, Maine 04462

HOURS: Daylight

TRAIL SYSTEM: Wilderness touring plus 24 kilometers (about 16 miles) of trails

TRAIL DIFFICULTY: All levels of challenge

TRAIL GROOMING: Tracked by snowmobile

RENTAL EQUIPMENT: Yes

INSTRUCTION: Yes, guides by appointment

FOOD FACILITIES: Yes, meals and snacks at the camp; cabins have full cooking facilities and there is a general store in camp

LODGING: Cabin lodging, with all the amenities—sauna, pool, and Jacuzzi

HOW TO GET THERE: Follow Route 95 north to the Medway exit, then to Mount Katahdin Road. Go through East Millinocket and Millinocket, then go 8¹/10 miles on Main Street, turn right onto Black Cat Road to the Robinson Twin Pine Camps sign.

This four season outdoor camp is set in one of the wildest and most beautiful New England settings, at the foot of Mount Katahdin, the second highest mountain in the Northeast (100 feet shorter than Mount Washington). Katahdin is set in Baxter Park Wilderness Preserve, with unlimited wilderness skiing and showshoeing in its quarter-million acres.

Skiers have 24 kilometers of trails that wind through all sorts of terrain and access to snowmobiles that can take them to the start of an infinite number of unbroken wilderness trips. This is a rugged North Woods setting, and yet the après-ski life has the comforts of the best of ski country, a large, open fire in the common room, good food and cheer, and a pool, Jacuzzi, and sauna. Other outdoor amenities include skating, sledding, tracking, and ice-fishing. A true outdoorsman's ski experience.

CARTER'S FARM AND CROSS-COUNTRY SKI CENTER

Route 26
Oxford, Maine 04270
(207) 539–4848

HOURS: 9:00 A.M. to 6:00 P.M. Night skiing on weekends

TRAIL SYSTEM: 25 kilometers (about 15 miles)

TRAIL DIFFICULTY: Easiest, more difficult

TRAIL GROOMING: Groomed and trackset; skating lanes

RENTAL EQUIPMENT: Yes; retail shop

INSTRUCTION: Yes

FOOD FACILITIES: Trail snacks at center; restaurants within a few miles

LODGING: Motels in South Paris and Otisfield, about 7 miles away. Bed-and-breakfast available at center

HOW TO GET THERE: Maine Turnpike through Portland, Maine, to Exit 11 at Gray. Route 100 to Route 26 north. The farm is about 12 miles from Gray.

So many of the most pleasant New England touring centers have been established on working farms, and this one is in that tradition. Carter's Farm Market is a summer produce operation which, once the snow flies, turns its gently rolling pastureland and woods into a full-scale touring center. The retail/rental facility is well stocked with skis, clothing, and equipment, and the lodge is a friendly place to relax and talk about what wax you should have used.

The trails at Carter's Farm are varied, from open-field cruisers and racing courses, to one lovely solitary tour along the Androscoggin River. Hogan's Pond is another pretty destination for a daily tour. At Carter's, citizen races are run throughout the season, along with junior programs and a Winter Carnival. Night skiing is also a fun feature of the area. David Carter, director of the area, is a cross-country skier with twenty-five years' experience who set up the Jackson Touring Center for Eastern Mountain Sports. When it comes to running a touring center, Carter knows what he is about.

RANGELEY MUNICIPAL TRAILS

Box 490
Rangeley, Maine 04970
(207) 864–5671

HOURS: 9:00 A.M. to 4:00 P.M.

TRAIL SYSTEM: 20 kilometers (12 miles)

TRAIL DIFFICULTY: Easiest, more difficult, most difficult

TRAIL GROOMING: As needed; 35 kilometers groomed; skating lanes

RENTAL EQUIPMENT: Yes

INSTRUCTION: PSIA-certified instructors; Telemark

FOOD FACILITIES: Available at the Saddleback Mountain base lodge

LODGING: Condominiums available at the mountain; inns and motels in the town nearby

HOW TO GET THERE: Maine Turnpike to Exit 12 in Auburn, Maine; Route 4 heading north to Rangeley; follow signs to Saddleback and the touring facility

As an Alpine area, Saddleback is rightfully dubbed New England's best-kept secret. The same can be said for the Nordic touring center and the region generally. It is a land of broad lakes—Rangeley, Saddleback, and Mooselookmeguntik—and trout streams that course out of the Bigelow Mountains, whose peaks command views of the entire region. Despite the beauty of the area and a base elevation (2,500 feet) that ensures a much longer-than-average ski season, the Rangeley region is uncrowded and unhurried. This is a perfect area to combine a Nordic-Alpine ski vacation, or to make use of Saddleback Mountain's easier Alpine trails for your Telemark work. The 40 kilometers of carefully groomed and trackset trails combine all the terrain, from gentle rolling tours along the lake shore and across the lake expanse, to stiff climbs up the flank of Saddleback Mountain itself. One reward for this climb is a truly stunning view of Saddleback Lake followed by a gentle meandering descent down the Lazy River trail. Then follow this with an après-ski hour in the Painted Pony, Saddleback's rollicking lounge upstairs at the base lodge. A full cafeteria operates daily here and serves a homemade chili that must, hands down, take top chili honors in all of ski land.

THE BIRCHES SKI TOURING CENTER

Rockwood, Maine 04478
(207) 534–7305

HOURS: Dawn to dusk

TRAIL SYSTEM: 40 kilometers (25 miles); unlimited wilderness

TRAIL DIFFICULTY: Easiest, more difficult, most difficult

TRAIL GROOMING: Groomed and trackset as needed

RENTAL EQUIPMENT: Yes

INSTRUCTION: PSIA-certified

FOOD FACILITIES: Restaurant in Rockwood Center, 2 miles from the center

LODGING: Several cabins and lodges in the area

HOW TO GET THERE: I–95 to Newport, Maine, then Route 7 going north to Dexter; Route 23 heading north to Guilford; pick up Routes 6 and 15 through the town of Greenville around the lake to Rockwood; cross the Moose River and follow a logging road to center

Looking for wilderness ski trips? Overnights? Fly-ins to the wild backcountry of the Northeast? Here it is. Maine's big North Woods is the closest thing in New England to rival Michigan's Upper Peninsula. This is not intended to scare off less-experienced skiers but simply to remind potential visitors that outback trekking in this countryside requires forethought, planning, and investigation. That said, the rewards of skiing The Birches are immense, and the sport enters an entirely new dimension.

The center itself overlooks Mt. Kineo, and skiers can be content to stay on the 40 kilometers of groomed, trackset trails along the picturesque western shore of the lake. There is a rental and retail shop, and hot drinks and sandwiches are available. For the adventurous, The Birches operates in conjunction with North Country Outfitters and can plan a multiday trek for skiers; the only requirements are good health and a willing heart. No experience is necessary, in other words. You will be in the hands of professional guides and instructors who will lead the tour through these stupendous backlands, leaving 2,000-foot towers like Elephant and Indian mountains at your back. During the day, you'll ski from inn to inn along old logging roads and woodland trails; late in the afternoon you'll be ready to relax around a warm stove before the big home-cooked dinner at the inn. A hot tub and sauna are also available for skiers after a day on the trail.

For the ultimate New England trek, The Birches offers a back-packing tour to Chimney Pond at the base of mile-high Mt. Katahdin. By day you'll be working over Alpine terrain—rock faces, ice falls, and snow fields. You'll learn the basics of winter moun-taineering and ski the lower snow bowls of the majestic Katahdin. This trip requires both physical and mental stamina, though not great skiing experience. The adventure is well worth the effort.

BLACK MOUNTAIN OF MAINE

50 Congress Street
Rumford, Maine 04276
(207) 364–8977

HOURS: Dawn to dusk, December through March

TRAIL SYSTEM: 15 kilometers (about 9 miles)

TRAIL DIFFICULTY: Easiest, more difficult, most difficult

TRAIL GROOMING: Groomed and trackset

RENTAL EQUIPMENT: Nearby in Rumford

INSTRUCTION: Yes

FOOD FACILITIES: A lunch counter at the center

LODGING: In Rumford

HOW TO GET THERE: Maine Turnpike north to Auburn; Route 4 to Livermore; Route 108 to Rumford

Black Mountain of Maine is a medium-sized area in the central range of the state, near an Alpine ski area and ski-jumping complex. The trail system was intelligently designed by Chammy Broomhall, designer of the Olympic trail system at Lake Placid and Squaw Valley, and still a vital part of the competitive Nordic scene. Black Mountain reflects this dedication to high-quality cross-country ski-ing on every level, from first-time-out novices to racers training for a Ski Chase marathon.

SKI-A-BIT
Route 112, Box 115
West Buxton, Maine 04093
(207) 929–4824

HOURS: 8:00 A.M. to dusk, Saturday and Sunday; 9:00 A.M. to dusk, Monday through Friday

TRAIL SYSTEM: 40 kilometers (about 25 miles)

TRAIL DIFFICULTY: Easiest to more difficult

TRAIL GROOMING: Groomed and trackset; skating trails available

RENTAL EQUIPMENT: Yes, including children's, about ninety sets

INSTRUCTION: Yes

FOOD FACILITIES: Snack area at Ski-A-Bit, plenty of restaurants nearby

LODGING: Plenty of lodging along Route 1

HOW TO GET THERE: Maine Turnpike (95) to exit 5; take the first right after the toll booth onto Industrial Park Road then left onto Route 112; Ski-A-Bit will be about 10 miles down Route 112 on the left

Ski-A-Bit is a family-owned operation. It offers 40 kilometers of cross-country ski trails that are groomed and trackset, with skating trails available. The trails average 12 feet in width. There are some good hills on the trails but none that are too difficult.

The terrain at Ski-A-Bit is mostly woodland trail and rolling hills. A few of the trails are steep and challenging with cranky turns on the downslopes. But all trails are well-marked as to trail difficulty.

After you've worn yourself out skiing and want to get a bite to eat, visit the snack bar. There's a warming shed with tables, or if you'd rather, there are picnic tables outside. If you're a nature buff, or even if you're not, check out the trees around the picnic tables; they are labeled with little signs.

Owner, Stan Hujsak makes it a point to go out with new skiers to get them comfortable with the sport. It's not a long outing, but he doesn't charge you either.

SMILING HILL FARM

781 County Road
Westbrook, Maine 04092
(207) 775–4818, ext. 19

HOURS: Daylight to sunset

TRAIL SYSTEM: 20 kilometers (about 12 miles)

TRAIL DIFFICULTY: Mostly easy to moderate, with some expert terrain

TRAIL GROOMING: Yes, tracked and groomed by snowmobile with a 6-foot skating lane

RENTAL EQUIPMENT: Yes

INSTRUCTION: Yes, by appointment

FOOD FACILITIES: A restaurant at the area serves light lunches and offers catered meals for groups

LODGING: Motels and inns throughout the Portland region

HOW TO GET THERE: Take Route 95 from Boston, then Maine Turnpike to Exit 8. Follow signs to Westbrook.

This 400-plus acre dairy farm in the southern Portland area of Maine offers 20 kilometers of tracked and groomed cross-country ski trails, with warming huts throughout the trail system. The farm is still a working dairy farm known for manufacturing its own ice cream. After working up that stoic feel of a day burning calories, blow it all at the dairy store on the farm.

As with most skiing through farmland, Smiling Hill is pretty much as its name suggests—gently rolling terrain and lots of flats through the pleasantly scenic meadows. While there is not too much here to really dazzle the expert skier looking for some life-on-the-edge, there is plenty of terrain and variety here to interest most family ski groups with varying abilities and wills.

Sleigh rides behind a team of Percheron draft horses, skating, and sledding round out the non-skiing activity at this mellow place. Its proximity to Portland (and Boston) make it convenient as well.

INDEX TO SKIING SITES

I

Inn at East Hill Farm, The (Troy, New Hampshire), 138

Inn at Quail Run (Wilmington, Vermont), 104

J

Jackson Ski Touring Foundation (Jackson, New Hampshire), 125

Jay Peak Ski Area (Jay, Vermont), 72

K

Katahdin Lake Wilderness Camps (Millinocket, Maine), 163

Kennedy Park (Lenox, Massachusetts), 41

L

Lincoln Guide Service (Lincoln, Massachusetts), 41

Little Lyford Pond Lodge (Brownville, Maine), 150

Loon Mountain Cross-Country Center (Lincoln, New Hampshire), 130

M

Maple Corner Farm Cross-Country Ski Area (Granville, Massachusetts), 38

Maplewood Farm (Norfolk, Connecticut), 30

Moose Mountain Lodge (Etna, New Hampshire), 118

Mount Abram Ski Touring (Locke Mills, Maine), 160

Mt. Mansfield Ski Touring Center (Stowe, Vermont), 91

Mount Washington Valley (Intervale, New Hampshire), 125

Mountain Meadows Cross-Country Ski Center (Killington, Vermont), 74

Mountain Top Cross-Country Ski Center (Chittenden, Vermont), 64

N

Natanis Cross-Country Ski Trails (Augusta, Maine), 145

Nordic Adventures (Rochester, Vermont), 88

Nordic Inn Ski Touring Center (Landgrove, Vermont), 75

Nordic Skier, The (Wolfeboro, New Hampshire), 140

Norsk Cross-Country Ski Center (New London, New Hampshire), 132

Northfield Mountain Ski Touring Center (Northfield, Massachusetts), 43

Notchview Reservation (Windsor, Massachusetts), 51

Also of Interest from The Globe Pequot Press

Classic Backcountry Skiing $12.95
    A Guide to the Best Ski Tours in New England

The Best Bike Rides In New England $12.95
    Forty-four inviting tours in the six New England states

Short Bike Rides In Connecticut $ 9.95
    Thirty-five tours through the Nutmeg State

Short Bike Rides In Rhode Island $10.95
    The best and most appealing tours through rural landscape

Short Bike Rides In Central And Western Massachusetts $12.95
    Forty-two rides, including six through the Berkshire mountains

Short Bike Rides In Eastern Massachusetts $14.95
    Seventy-six tours around Boston and the shores

Short Bike Rides On Cape Cod, Nantucket And The Vineyard $ 9.95
    Newest edition covers the beauty of these picturesque routes

Sixty Selected Short Nature Walks In Connecticut $ 9.95
    Interesting and colorful walks in their natural beauty

Short Nature Walks On Cape Cod And The Vineyard $ 8.95
    Escape the crowd with these twenty-six quiet, beautiful walks

Quiet Water Canoe Guide: MA, CT and RI $12.95
    For the beginner as well as the most experienced paddler

Budget Dining And Lodging In New England $12.95
    Four hundred restaurants, B&B's and motels

Recommended Country Inns New England $14.95
    Gracious hospitality in a country ambiance

Bed & Breakfast in New England $16.95
    Delightful country lodgings

Available from your bookstore or directly from the publisher. For a free catalogue or to place an order, call toll free, 24 hours a day, 1-800-243-0495, or write to The Globe Pequot Press, P.O. Box 833, Old Saybrook, Connecticut 06475-0833.